Assemblies
to teach
Golden Rules

MARGARET GOLDTHORPE
and LUCY UNDERWOOD

before the

The rights of Margaret Goldthorpe and Lucy Underwood to be identified as the authors of this work have
been asserted by them in accordance with sections 77 and 78 of the Copyright, Designs and Patents Act
1988.

Assemblies to teach Golden Rules
LL01235
ISBN 1 85503 310 0
© Margaret Goldthorpe and Lucy Underwood
All rights reserved
First published 2000
Reprinted 2001, 2002
New edition 2005

Printed in the UK for LDA
Abbeygate House, East Road, Cambridge, CB1 1DB UK

Contents

Acknowledgements

It is always good to be given the opportunity to say thank you. We should like to say thanks to:

Dennis Goldthorpe, Headteacher of Alexandra Special School in Harrow, whose contribution is not only that he invented some of these assemblies but also that he encouraged in Alexandra School a belief that assemblies should be huge fun, yet needle sharp.

All of the staff and children of Alexandra School for their help and inspiration over the years.

Dorothy Dale, Headteacher of Marlborough First & Middle School, and to all the children there, for their practical support and encouragement.

Annie Wynne-Morgan for prayerful help.

Celia German for composing and writing the delightful Golden Rules song.

Linda Anderson for the Truly Messy One with the Pancakes.

Evelyn Glennie, for the kind permission to use her name.

Our long-suffering friends, who have all agreed to trial whatever bizarre suggestions we have thrown at them, usually late on a Sunday night.

Our patient editor Jo Browning Wroe and her supportive assistant Liam.

Jenny Mosley, for the Quality Circle Time Model.

But, above all, we should like to thank our families, who have given us the freedom to work on this book and the encouragement to complete it.

Margaret Goldthorpe and Lucy Nutt
Sarratt Bottom, May 2000

Preface

One of the most powerful gifts you can give to your school is a vision. To be clear in your head about how you want the school to be and where you want it to go is wonderful. Holding clear such a vision for each child is indeed precious.

Having Golden Rules gives you such a vision, for the school and for each person it nurtures – for the Golden Rules reinforced throughout this book are not 'doing rules' of the 'Do not wear trainers' variety. Rather, they are moral values.

They are not a vision of the routines you want your children to keep to, instead they are a vision of the people you want them to be.

The assemblies in this book also support the Quality Circle Time Model. The Golden Rules are, in many ways, at the heart of this model. They are the moral values which underpin all of the choices and decisions made by the school and its pupils.

The Quality Circle Time Golden Rules are:

> We are gentle – We don't hurt others
> We are kind and helpful – We don't hurt anybody's feelings
> We listen – We don't interrupt
> We are honest – We don't cover up the truth
> We work hard – We don't waste our own or others' time
> We look after property – We don't waste or damage things

These rules need to be displayed on every classroom and corridor wall, in the back of the home–school link books and even outside on the playground walls. Having a set of Golden Rules or moral values is useless, however, if we allow them to become nothing more than a bunch of good intentions stuck on the walls.

We need to get these moral values off the walls and into the children's hearts.

We don't need our children to say, 'I know I'm supposed to be gentle', but rather, 'I know I am gentle. OK, not always. But I know when I am being gentle and I like myself. I know when I'm not and it makes me feel pretty uncomfortable.'

We need them to understand themselves as people who are kind and helpful, honest, hard working, careful and good listeners.

We want our schools to be places where being gentle, kind, honest, hard working, careful and a good listener is valued and encouraged. We don't want them to be places where people know how they should behave, but still do exactly whatever suits them best at the time.

We want them to be places where everyone learns to 'walk the talk'.

It is a good vision.

How are we to do this?

One of the most important ways is for the children to come to a personal understanding of how to live the rules through discussion in Quality Circle Time.

For a more detailed discussion on Quality Circle Time, I refer you to the books listed in the Resources section at the back of this book.

An equally important way is to remember to catch children getting things right and then praise them. If we all praise children using words of the Golden Rules, then everyone within the school community will be reinforcing the same message. There will be consistency; everyone is using the same language, singing from the same song sheet. We will be helping each child to get a clear and unambiguous picture of themselves as someone who is helpful, honest, hard working, gentle and careful and who pays attention.

No more are there six million rules in the world. There are only six – the same six for everyone. There might be a million ways to break them, and a million ways to keep them, but there are still only six rules; and every man, woman and child in the building knows what they are and can point out with pleasure exactly when anyone is getting it right!

That is not vague and woolly praise but accurate affirmation, enabling you to be alive to the best impulses and actions of the children.

What is more, when these Golden Rules are used and owned by the whole community, then every single member of staff – teaching, learning support, catering, lunchtime, clerical, ancillary, everyone – is doing the same. Each is using the words of the rules, each is living under the same umbrella of the same rules.

All are helping each other and the children to know themselves for their best selves – to know and become that vision of themselves that we have for them. This is where assemblies come in. For we are discussing vision and moral values, and these are deep and precious things.

Assembly is a time for coming together and discussing what should be closest to our hearts. We need to think about how we can understand ourselves well enough to be able to be the best people we can be. And how through such an awareness we can learn to behave towards other people as we should like them to behave towards us.

If you have an assembly once a week where these values are shared with the children, explored, discussed and moved into a place of deeper understanding and greater ownership, then your vision can truly be said to be the vision of the whole school.

That is the purpose of these assemblies.

Note that for each assembly there is a prayer and a 'Thought for the day'. Both have been included so that you can choose whether or not to address God, as appropriate for your school.

A spoonful of sugar

Golden Rule

We are kind and helpful – We don't hurt anybody's feelings.

Preparation

Hardly any.

You will need:

- a bottle of lemon juice or a plastic lemon containing juice,
- a jug of water and a glass,
- a jar of runny honey *or* a bowl of sugar, and a spoon.

If you have any nightlights in jars you could light several for this assembly. You could even have lots of candles and shut the curtains and dim the lights.

The assembly

This is a thoughtful assembly about how we can be loving towards those who, for whatever reason, are hard to love.

You have probably heard the song 'A spoonful of sugar helps the medicine go down.' What does it mean?

Well, it means that if you have to swallow a spoonful of nasty medicine, it can help take the taste away if you follow it up with a spoonful of something sweet, like honey or jam or lemon curd.

That's what it means literally. But it can also mean that something sweet can take away bitterness. Imagine it like this ...

This glass of water is your life. It's OK, no problems, it tastes fine.

> *Get a volunteer to sip it, just a sip!*

But sometimes bad things happen that can make our lives not so pleasant.

Perhaps one of your grandparents dies. That's very bad.

> *Shake or squirt lots of lemon juice into the glass of water – don't get the volunteer to taste the water again until the end.*

Or maybe your mum and dad decide not to live with each other any more. *(More lemon juice.)* This can be very sad for a while.

Or maybe it's not as bad as those things, but it's still really sad. Perhaps a pet dies. *(More lemon juice.)*

Or maybe you have lots of problems making and keeping friends at school. *(More lemon juice.)*

Sometimes the things that go wrong just seem bad to us. For example, we may start to find school work harder and it worries us. Perhaps we slowly realise we are finding reading a problem or sums are getting difficult. *(More lemon juice.)*

> *Use any examples you may feel are pertinent to your school, each time adding a squirt of lemon juice.*

Sad things are like lemon juice in the water. They can make life taste bitter. Now the glass of water won't taste quite so pleasant. In fact, it might cause us to make a face, sometimes quite a nasty face.

Like this … *(Get your volunteer to sip the water. It should have enough lemon juice in it to make them wince!)* What does it taste like now?

I think we all know people who have faces that always look a bit sour and cross. Maybe that's because they have lives that taste a bit sour. And sometimes their words are rather sharp, too. What can we do to help?

Well, we can remember the Golden Rule 'We are kind and helpful.'

We can make an extra special effort to love them. *(Put a little sugar or runny honey into the glass of lemon juice and stir.)*

We can smile at them. *(More sugar or honey.)*

We can help them out with their work. *(More sugar.)*

We can listen to them. *(More.)*

We can be gentle to them and ask them to play with us. *(More sugar or honey.)*

We can make sure we don't behave in a sharp way back, even if they are a bit sharp to us. *(More sugar.)*

We can speak gently. *(More sugar.)*

So we have to be there to be a friend. By doing that we are like sugar or honey in the lemon juice. We can add a little sweetness to their life. *(Get the volunteer to sip the water now.)*

Then it doesn't taste bad any more. Maybe they will even have a sweeter face and speak softer words.

So what are we adding to a bitter life to make it sweet?

Love. And each of us can do the loving.

You might like to practise silence here, perhaps light candles and dim the lights. Suggest everyone is silent for half a minute while they think about someone they could be kinder to. (Half a minute is quite long enough; it will seem a long time.) Ask them to make a silent promise to themselves to be more loving to that person.

Prayer

Dear Lord, help us to be loving friends. Give us the wisdom to see when people are having a hard time and give us lots of help so we can be kind to them. If they are a bit sharp to us give us the strength not to behave in a sharp way back. Help us to remember that a gentle word can turn away anger. Amen.

Thought for the day

Let us try to think of how other people may be feeling before we judge them. Let us remember that our kindness can be their strength.

Bible verses

Romans 15, v2; 12, v15
Galatians 6, v2
Proverbs 17, v17; 15, v1

Much of the New Testament is relevant. So is the story of Ruth – especially Ruth 1, v16–17.

I'm glad I'm not a domino

Golden Rule

We are gentle – We don't hurt others.

Preparation

You will need:

- a table,
- a box of dominoes,
- 2 'plants' in the audience (children or teachers; it's actually funnier if the plants are teachers), one to come up and look at the dominoes and accidentally knock them over, the second to defend the first.

For the follow-up you will need some black sugar paper and a box of large, round, white, self-adhesive spots.

The assembly

At the beginning of the assembly stand the dominoes up in a line. Talk to the children as you do it. Explain that you want to make a good line, but it's very fragile because if one domino falls over, they will all fall over.

When they are all standing in a line, ask the first 'plant' to come up and look at them. As they look, say, 'Don't touch' and 'Be careful' etc.

Suddenly the person 'accidentally' knocks them over. They all go down one after the other.

Now you have to pretend to get mad!

You: **You have spoiled my dominoes! If you hadn't been so careless I'd still have a tidy line. It took me ages to put them up. Right, I'm going to have to punch you on the nose!**

Plant 2 (stands up in the audience): **Oh no, you don't. That's not fair. It was an accident. They didn't mean to do it. If you punch them I'll punch you back.**

All three of you square up to one another, doing a bit of pushing and shoving and making threatening noises of the 'OK, then let's fight' and 'Right, if that's want you want, that's fine by me' sort. If you want to, you can brief another teacher or the caretaker to join in at this point, doing a bit of "ere, wot you doin' to my mate, I'll 'ave to sort you out' acting.

After a minute or two of this (and do ham it up, really play for laughs), suddenly say: 'STOP!' You all stop.

You: **This could get a great deal worse. Before long this could be a major fight. Someone could get really hurt. Half the people involved won't even know what it's about. Let's sit down now.**

Everyone sits down.

Now explain what the play was about.

Fights are like these dominoes. Once one starts, then other people go on getting involved and things snowball, going from bad to worse. How can we stop the dominoes falling?
- Don't knock them?
- Don't touch them?

Once they start to go it is more or less impossible to stop them falling down.

What is the difference between us and the dominoes? We can call 'Stop' at any time. We can say:

- 'This is silly, let's not fight.'
- 'It's OK. I know it was an accident. Let's not fight.'
- 'This isn't worth falling out about. Let's do something else.'

What rule do we have to remember?

It's 'We are gentle – We don't hurt others.'

Because we aren't like dominoes:
- We can't say, 'Don't touch each other' – because we will.
- We can't say, 'Don't bump into each other' – because we will.
- We can't say, 'Don't ever do anything to annoy each other' – because we will.

We are human beings, not bits of wood or plastic.

What we can do is to choose how we respond, because we are not bits of wood or plastic. We can stop the chain reaction.

We can say, even if we are the injured party, 'Stop. This is silly. Let's go and play something else. I know it was an accident. It's not worth fighting about.'

And the dominoes stop falling.

So, remember, when trouble starts:
- You are not a domino!
- You are a person who knows it is right to be gentle and who can stop the trouble.
- You can choose how you respond!

If you find that hard to remember, you can remember this rhyme:

> **I'm glad I'm not a domino,**
> **Indeed, I think it's good**
> **That I'm a real person**
> **And not a piece of wood.**

Prayer

Dear Lord, whenever there is arguing help us to remember that we can choose how to respond. Give us the strength to stop and make a choice and give us the wisdom to make the right choice. Help us to remember that you told us the only guide we need in knowing how to behave towards others is that we are to love them. Amen.

Thought for the day

Let us never forget that we always have a choice in how we behave. Let us use the Golden Rules as our guide when making those decisions.

Follow-up

You might like to follow this up throughout the next week. We have found the following works well.

Draw a series of dominoes on paper or card, each about 18 cm x 11 cm (make maybe 8 of them).

Pin them onto a backed noticeboard in a central place in school. Put the verse in the middle and the dominoes around it.

Tell the children that every time they are aware that they have stopped and thought about how to respond to a situation and made a calmer choice, they can come and write (or have written for them) their name on a white spot and stick it onto a domino.

In a week's time, bring all the dominoes to assembly. Ask some of the children whose names are on the dominoes to tell everyone what their problem had been and how they had responded in a gentle way, stopping the dominoes falling. Give them lots of praise, claps, stickers or certificates.

Bible verses

Proverbs 16, v32; 19, v11
John 13, v35

The two-headed hyena

Golden Rule

We listen – We don't interrupt.

Preparation

This assembly needs very little preparation.

Chose your hyena carefully. You will need two children who are not afraid to act and can pull some good faces. You will also need:

- a simple headband with paper ears,
- a piece of cloth for the hyena to wear and for you to tear,
- 2 large pieces of paper and pens (to be given to 2 reasonably good spellers).

This assembly has two conclusions, one fairly simple, the second more complex. You can use your own judgement about whether you want to include the more complicated conclusion.

The assembly

This is what you tell the school:

Today's Golden Rule is 'We listen'. I was told this story by a friend of mine and we almost had a serious falling out over it. You see, I didn't bother to try to understand what she was really telling me. I think you'll see why I went wrong when you hear how this story starts.

'Once upon a time there was a two-headed hyena.'

Well, I ask you, a two-headed hyena! Already I didn't believe it. This hyena lived in the desert and was starving. It hadn't eaten for about three days.

> *At this point bring on the two children who are acting the part of the two-headed hyena.*

Who has a favourite food?

> *Get several suggestions and vote for the two most popular ones. It will probably be pizza and chocolate. Write the names of the two foods on the paper. Then get children to hold these make-shift banners up on opposite sides of the hall. The poor, hungry hyena meanwhile can be asleep in the middle.*

It was day 4 of the hyena's hunger and it hadn't had much to eat for a long time. It woke up and this head *(point to one child)* could smell the tantalising smell of hot pizza.

At the same time, this head *(point to the other child)* could smell the most luscious chocolate. Both heads set off in opposite directions after the food they could smell.

Problem. Neither could move.

They sat back and looked at each other. This head started to howl because it wanted the pizza, this head howled because it wanted the chocolate.

> *Let them howl for as long as you can stand it! Then stop them.*

Over here, this head *(pointing)* was feeling very hungry and it could still smell the delicious pizza. He was so hungry he thought he could hear the pizza calling to him. *(Get the children near the pizza poster to whisper 'Pizza, pizza, pizza'.)*

This head *(pointing)* was so hungry, it could hear the scrumptious chocolate calling. *(Get the children near the chocolate banner to whisper 'Chocolate, chocolate, chocolate'.)*

The hyena was in a frenzy, pulling, tugging against itself – sometimes going round in circles. *(Get the hyena to dodge from side to side.)*

This carried on and on until ...

> *Tear the piece of fabric down the middle and tell the children to fall down dead. All the whisperers must stop then, too.*

The hyena never made it to any food.

Our Golden Rule talks about listening. Did the hyena heads listen?

No, they shouted or howled one another down. If they had stopped to listen to each other, they could have had both the pizza and the chocolate. But they didn't. The two-headed hyena died.

The second conclusion goes as follows:

That is one kind of listening. At the end of this story, my friend was still saying that she believed this story was true. 'Look,' I said, 'nice story, but it isn't true.'

But she insisted that it was. Back and forth we argued until I realised that I was being no better than the hyena. Finally, instead of just shouting her down, I asked her how it could be true.

'Because it is true that greed can be dangerous, as it was to the hyena.'

I hadn't listened to that particular message that she had been trying to tell me. No, she didn't really believe in two-headed hyenas, but she did believe in the message the story told. For me there are two meanings to this story. One is about straightforward listening and not speaking too soon, and one is about listening and thinking about what you have heard.

Someone famous once said, 'Seek first to understand and then to be understood.' Maybe we should listen to what the other person is really saying and not be so busy trying to get our point across.

Prayer

Dear Lord, so many arguments start because people do not listen to each other. Help us to listen to the thoughts and opinions of others. Help us also to listen for you speaking to us in times of thoughtfulness and quiet, and through the wise words of people around us. Amen.

Thought for the day

Let us remember to listen to the words others say. Let us think about the meanings and beliefs that the words tell us, without rushing in too soon.

Bible verses

Psalms 46, v10; 4, v3
1 John 4, v11

Let our best selves shine through

Golden Rule

We work hard — We don't waste our own or others' time.

Preparation

You will need two pieces of old brass or silver. (It is assumed that you will be using brass.) One must be tarnished. One must be pre-cleaned, bright and shiny. If you are stuck for these, charity shops usually have a good cheap collection of old bells, dishes, plates etc.

You will also need a can of Brasso and a soft cloth (a bit of torn-up old sheet, pillowcase or vest would be fine.)

The assembly

Tell the children that today we are going to talk about working hard, not just at our school work, but working hard at being our best selves.

Show them the two prepared pieces. Explain that one is tarnished and looks a bit of a mess, but underneath the dirt and tarnish it is still as beautifully shiny as it was on the day the craftsman made it.

Explain clearly that when it was new, it was shiny and glowing. But, if we don't do anything to something made of brass, it will gradually become tarnished.

At this point begin polishing the item with the Brasso and the cloth. Continue polishing as you speak.

Explain that we are a bit like brass. Inside each of us is our good, beautiful, shiny self, just as bright and shiny as the day we were made. But staying that way is hard work. Whenever we give in to our worst selves and:

- muck around in class rather than work,
- forget to write down our homework properly,
- do five minutes' homework instead of doing it properly,
- join in with backbiting or gossipping,

then we are not trying hard to be our best selves and we are allowing ourselves to become tarnished.

But at any time we can stop this and change. We can start working on being our best selves. We can start polishing! We can:

- remember to present our work as well as possible,
- walk away from – rather than towards – trouble,
- keep watch over what we say and refrain from gossip,
- try to help other people at all times.

Ask the children for things they think they could do.

Each time we do this we give our best selves a bit of a polish. It takes a lot more effort than just giving in to the easy way and letting ourselves get tarnished, but the benefits are enormous.

By now you should have a shiny candlestick, bell, jug or whatever.

We will have come back to being our best selves. Of course, we will have to keep working at it, because if we stop we will gradually get dull and tarnished again.

But remember – every time you do something that is right, you give the candlestick *(or whatever the item you are using is)* another polish.

It's hard work being our best selves, but it's worth it. We are all beautiful and shiny underneath and hard work will keep us that way.

Prayer

Dear God, you know the bright person that you made us to be. Let us be wholehearted and constant in our efforts to shine, for you and each other. Amen.

Thought for the day

What can we do today to polish our best selves?

Bible verses

Colossians 3, v22–23
Galatians 6, v9–10
Ephesians 6, v6–7
Proverbs 21, v23

Follow-up

After this assembly you can keep the candlestick (or whatever item you used) in your office. When miscreants are sent to you, you can give them the candlestick, the cloth and the Brasso and set them to work polishing. When they have finished, praise them, saying they have worked hard and made the dull old candlestick come back to its beautiful, best self. Then send them away, telling them they can do the same for themselves if they work really hard at their work/behaviour/friendships (whatever the problem was). Then they too will be able to show the world their best self.

Extra assembly point

If yours is a church school, you can run the assembly as described, but finish slightly differently. Make sure the tarnished item is a candlestick that will hold a large candle.

Once you have polished the candlestick and drawn the conclusion, you can set the candlestick on a table in front of the whole school. Place a big candle in it and light it.

Now you can tell them that the flame is God's love for us. Christians believe if we work hard at being our best selves we will reflect that light for all to see.

However, if we allow ourselves to be dull and tarnished through idleness and complacency, then, although God's love will still shine over us, we will not reflect it. People will not be able to see God's love reflected in us.

We should shine and be our best selves. That is what we are supposed to do.

The story of the honest draper

(and the dubious carrot salesperson)

Golden Rule

We are honest – We don't cover up the truth.

Preparation

A Muslim friend told me this story. I don't know its provenance. It tackles a subject that some children find hard. This assembly can be very colourful.

You need:

- a length of floaty material (try to use a light sari, which can be wafted around beautifully),
- some carrots.

You could spend some time organising this assembly in advance with a group of children, but it can be done on the hoof by giving children small prompt cards.

If necessary, you could just tell the story of the honest draper.

The assembly

I need a couple of volunteers *(pause)* who are prepared to do some tasting of chocolate. Yes, I thought I'd have lots of people wanting this job.

Choose two or three children and call them up to the front or into the middle, depending on how your assemblies are arranged. Produce the carrots.

Sorry, that was a lie. It doesn't matter, does it? You're going to be tasting carrots. Right, try this carrot. Not bad, was it?

> *While the children are eating the first carrot, ask who likes carrots, who eats organic food at home etc.*

OK, next one. Compare it to the taste of the first carrot. It was better than the first, wasn't it? Well, you see, it was organic.

> *Get the children to agree that it tasted better. If you have a bright spark trying to say it was the same, agree with them and go on to the next bit; all you have to emphasise is the word 'was'.*

Actually, that *was* another lie. Both those carrots were the same. But it didn't matter. If I hadn't told you, you wouldn't have known.

> *Let the children sit down.*

Does it matter if I told a lie? No one would have known. Did it really matter?

> *Put in pauses so the children think about these questions. With older children it might be worth taking a vote before and after the following story, about whether it matters or not. A good assessment of the effectiveness of your assembly is if the number changes at the end of the story. On the other hand, you may not feel brave enough to test that.*

> *At this point, if you have rehearsed some children in the story of the honest draper, ask them to come up to the front. If not, collect three volunteers: one shopper, one assistant and the boss. Alternatively, you can just tell the story.*

The owner of a drapers shop needed a holiday. He had been working so hard.

> *A good actor could ham up looking haggard.*

He had the chance to go off on a day trip to the coast. Plenty of bingo, sticks of rock, ice cream, donkey rides and all the rest. Blissful. Unfortunately, there was one snag. Does anyone here have a shop in the family or know friends with a shop? What happens when the shopkeeper goes on holiday? The shop closes, unless, like this shop owner, you have a trusted assistant.

> *Get the assistant to come in. The owner mimes showing the assistant a few things in the shop.*

The assistant noticed a splendid piece of fabric hidden at the back of the shop.

> *At this point the children can pull out the material (or sari) and waft it to and fro.*

The boss explained that there was a fault in this beautiful piece of material and that either it could not be sold, or it could only be sold at half price. It couldn't be sold at full price.

> *The assistant nods and both children examine the sari intently.*

Off went the boss for a day's dissipation at the seaside. The assistant had a great time in the shop, sold some material, had a really good gossip with a friend who came in, ate a leisurely lunch – until through the door came ...

> *The shopper comes in, looks round and notices the lovely material. She goes over to it.*

Now this person had a very grand party to go to, and wanted a stunning dress. This material was just what she wanted. What should the assistant do? Should the assistant say the material actually had a fault in it or should he say nothing and sell it at full price?

> *Stop and repeat this question to the children. Find out what they would do.*

Well, the assistant decided to keep quiet. He thought that the owner would be delighted that the full price of the material had been paid.

At the end of the day the boss came back, stuffed with candy floss and hot dogs. He'd had a great day, and naturally he asked about what had gone on in the shop. The assistant told the boss the wonderful news. The faulty material had been sold at full price.

But, instead of being delighted at this news, the boss was furious.

What would all of you do, if you were in the boss's shoes?

> *Compare these answers to the ones you had earlier.*

The boss went out of his way to find the shopper, explained that there had been a mistake and gave her half her money back. Why did he do that?

> *From these answers pull together an understanding that there is such a thing as an internal standard of behaviour.*

Honesty does not always have to be obvious to anyone else. The shopkeeper followed his conscience and the teaching from the Koran to guide his behaviour. To him there was no doubt that he had to be honest and not cover up the truth. He had to tell the woman exactly what she had bought, and give her back half of her money.

Go back to the carrots.

Some lies are revealed very quickly. You could see very quickly that a carrot was not chocolate. The shopper would eventually have found out that there was a fault in the material. But you don't know even now if one carrot is organic or not.

All you have to go on is what you know of me. You have to trust my words by what you know of my character – my integrity. You know that I don't lie, I know that I don't lie. Even if I know no one will ever find me out, I still don't tell lies. Just like the draper, I believe it is wrong to lie.

I believe we have to be honest, always. Even to ourselves. Honesty starts inside us – first we must know that we always tell the truth even if we know we would never get found out.

Then, when we say something, others will know we always tell the truth and know us for an honest person. We can then trust ourselves and others can trust us.

Prayer

Dear God, help us not to live dishonestly in any way. A lie does not only live on our tongue but also in our hearts. Keep our hearts clean and our tongues honest. Amen.

Thought for the day

Let us know when we are telling the truth and when we are not. Let us not lie to ourselves or say that some lies are acceptable. We know that lies are never acceptable. Choosing the right path to be the best person that we can be is complicated, but let us listen to our conscience and allow that to guide us.

Bible verses

Proverbs 12, v22
Ephesians 4, v25
Psalms 119, v29; 19, v14

Treasure

Golden Rule

We look after property – We don't waste or damage things.

Preparation

This assembly needs some thought. You may be the kind of magpie-like person who has all sorts of odds and ends at home that will work for this. You may need to beg or borrow the stuff from friends and family.

You need:

- 4 boxes with lids (plastic boxes are fine),
- some tissue to cover items in the box,
- an expensive-looking object (I used a fake diamond brooch),
- a credit card or cheque book (I used a just-expired credit card),
- an expensive-looking watch (I used one from a Malaysian market),
- a clearly inexpensive piece of jewellery or ornament (I used a straw hat brooch).

Write the numbers 1 to 4 on the boxes.

Put one thing into each box. Cover each item with scrunched-up tissue.

Write down the number of the most valuable box on a piece of paper and seal it in an envelope. The item that is obviously the cheapest must be the one you value the most. The straw hat brooch was my most valuable item.

The assembly

Tell the children that you will be asking them to tell you which rule this assembly is about at the end of it. Begin the assembly by saying that there are some things of different value in the boxes. Give the sealed envelope to a child to keep safely.

Ask volunteers to come up one by one, open the boxes and tell the other children what is in the box. Once all the boxes are open, ask the four children to hold their boxes and arrange themselves in order, from the most to the least valuable. Ask the other children to think what order they would put the boxes in. Once they have sorted themselves out, ask someone to come and rearrange the boxes into the order they think is right. Then ask more children to do the same. Ask the children to vote for the most valuable object.

Ask the child with the envelope to come forward. Open it. The children will discover that your most valuable object is apparently the least valuable.

I then put the boxes into the order of least to most valuable to me. (You might want to do this; it depends on what your objects are.) I explained that the hat brooch had been given to me by a child in the very first class that I taught. The other things might be worth more money, but they could be replaced. The brooch could not be replaced.

Ask the children which rule this assembly illustrates. Explain that you never know what things other people value. You should never fiddle with or break things belonging to other people because you do not know what they mean to that person. Sometimes the oddest things have to be looked after. You need to keep this rule so that you do not unwittingly break the rules about being kind and gentle.

Prayer

Dear Lord, you hold each one of us carefully in your hands. We are all special to you. Teach us to value each other and to care for the things that other people hold dear. Amen.

Thought for the day

We are fortunate to have everything that we need. We must be responsible about the possessions that we and others have, and make sure that nothing is wasted or broken.

Bible verses

Deuteronomy 8, v6–14

You can change the world!

(bit by bit, step by step, doing what you can!)

Golden Rule

We look after property – We don't waste or damage things.

Preparation

You will need:

- a KitKat (or something similar),
- a newspaper,
- a can of drink (almost all of the contents drunk, to save you having to swig down a whole can of drink in the assembly),
- a wastepaper bin,
- a comfortable chair.

Have the chair and the wastepaper bin already set up in front of the school.

Photocopy the text for the assembly and stick it onto the newspaper so you can pretend to read the newspaper whilst in fact reading what is set out below.

The assembly

You come into the assembly carrying the drink and the KitKat and with the newspaper under your arm. Sit down in front of the school in the chair. Get out the newspaper and read as follows:

Today there is a large conference in Washington in the United States. All of the heads of state have gathered to discuss the future of the planet. There is considerable anxiety amongst all nations about the damage being done to the planet due to pollution.

You look up and address the school:

Isn't that worrying? It's true, there is a lot of pollution in the world. It's enough to give you sleepless nights.

Open the KitKat and throw the wrapper onto the floor. Continue reading:

There is also great anxiety about the use and waste of non-renewable resources.

Look up and explain:

That means things like oil and coal and things we use to make tin and glass. That is a great worry, too. I worry at night about what will happen when it all runs out.

Drink the contents of the can and throw the empty can in the wastepaper bin. Continue reading:

There is also a great deal of anxiety about pollution from cars.

Look up and say:

That's true. My sister and I went for a drive last week and we were talking about just that problem. I know people who get asthma from car pollution. And the traffic is terrible. I was trying to drive to my friend's house the other day and it was only half a mile but it took me three-quarters of an hour to get there! The traffic was so terrible. It cost me a fortune in petrol. I thought I would have a heart attack, I got so cross in that traffic jam. And it's causing holes in the ozone layer.

What will happen to the planet if it goes on like this? What will the world be like in a hundred years? I worry so much about the future.

This newspaper here is full of so many things. Such terrible news. Floods, famines, wars, holes in the ozone layer. And what can I do? Except worry. Oh, I *do* worry. It's all so terrible.

Stand up and throw the newspaper in the bin.

I'll have to stop thinking about it or I'll go mad. I mean, there is nothing *I* can do.

Go to walk off. Stop. Turn round and face the school.

Or is there? Is there something I can do? Tell me and … *(name a member of staff)* will write it down.

The responses can either be written down on a piece of paper or on an OHP.

You now need to get them to tell you to do such things as these:

- Pick up the wrapper and throw it in the bin to help the litter problem.
- Take the can to a can bank so that non-renewable resources can be recycled.
- Recycle the newspaper.
- Walk, not drive, to your friend's house (it was only half a mile), which will save energy and prevent you having a heart attack.
- Go for a walk or bicycle ride with your sister, instead of a needless drive.
- Have a fund-raising event for Oxfam or Save the Children or some other organisation that helps the victims of floods, earthquakes, famines etc.

When all this is completed, tell the school this:

Do you know, I feel much happier now? I feel much better knowing I am going to be doing something to make the world a better place and I'm not just worrying about things that are outside my control.

Do you ever do that? It's easy, isn't it, to get worried about things we see on the news that we can do nothing about? And then it's easy not to bother to do the things we could do to help.

If we all do all the small things we can to help, we will set a good example and maybe others will join us. And if everyone does all the small things they can do to help, these will add up to big things.

Prayer

Dear Lord, help us to have the courage to change the things we can change, the patience to endure the things we can't and the wisdom to know the difference. Amen.

or

Dear Lord, you have said that if we live as you have told us to, then you will help us. Help us to remember that. Amen.

Thought for the day

Let us never forget to do the things we can do that will help our friends and neighbours and our world. Let us remember that by changing ourselves and doing the little things we can help to make a big difference.

Bible verses

Matthew 25, v31–46; 6, v33

Turning over a new leaf

Golden Rules

We work hard – We don't waste our own or others' time.

Preparation

You don't need much for this assembly so it's good for a quick, last-minute, 'Omigosh-it's-my-assembly' assembly. You just need:

- a desk and chair,
- a volunteer,
- a very old book, as old as you can find,
- pen and paper.

The assembly

Show the school the old book. Point out to them that it looks different from new ones. Explain that the pages would have been individually typeset. If it is old enough, show them that the pages would have been cut by hand.

Say that the earliest books were written by hand, involving even more work.

Explain that pages of old books were called 'leaves'. If someone made a mistake whilst handwriting an old manuscript they would have to start again. They would have to 'turn over a new leaf' – make a fresh start, trying to avoid another mistake. These days we use the expression 'to turn over a new leaf' to mean much the same if we want to make a fresh start. We may want to try to work harder or behave better or eat more healthily.

But – it's not always easy. You need people to help you to turn over a new leaf. If you are to be successful you need help.

Call out your volunteer. Seat the child at the desk, facing the school. Put the pen and paper in front of them.

Explain that this child has decided to 'turn over a new leaf' and:

- work hard in class,
- be kind in the playground,
- give up eating unhealthy food at break time (or lunch), and
- stop talking about people.

Now present a playlet, with you as the bad guy and bad influence. You can really enjoy this. Use all the current slang and behave exactly as the children would in this situation. Await the laughs.

You, to the child at the desk: **Are you going to work hard in class, then?**

Child: **Yes.**

You: **What! Do you want to be a boff or something? Everyone will think you've turned sad if you do that. Come over here and look at these Pokemon cards I've brought in. *(Or refer to whatever is the current craze and use the current slang.)***

Child: **Oh, all right then.**

You: **At last! We are going out to play. Hey, come over here! What's the matter with you? We are going to have a bit of fun with that fat kid from Year 4.**

Child: **No thanks.**

You: **What? Don't you want to play? Do you think you're better than us or something? You are one sad loser. Come on.**

Child: **Oh, OK, then.**

Repeat this with food (e.g. tempting them to eat crisps or chew gum) and then with gossip, persuading them to get involved with a slanderous conversation.

You can choose two or three different volunteers. You can also adapt the scenario to be more pertinent to your school. The general idea is to tempt the child away from their resolution to do better. You can go over the top and behave like a thoroughly bad influence.

After this, return the volunteer(s) to the audience. Say to the school:

> You see, they wanted to turn over a new leaf, but to be successful they needed me to be kind and helpful to them. And I wasn't. Instead, I was unkind and tried to tempt them back to their old ways.
>
> If you are going to turn over a new leaf you must:
> - tell people what you are going to do (publish your intentions),
> - ask for someone to be a friend (a buddy) to help you,
> - trust that others will help you.
>
> This is where the rest of us come in. If we know someone is trying to turn over a new leaf, we must help them. Just as it wouldn't be kind if you kept offering a person on a diet something they were not supposed to eat, it isn't kind to tempt people who are trying to change.
>
> We must remember we have to help each other to be successful. Our help is vital to others' success.
>
> They *(pointing to the volunteer)* wanted to turn over a new leaf. They will have to **work hard**.
>
> But I *(pointing to yourself)* must remember that for them to be successful I must be **kind and helpful**. Remember, we are a community and we must each help each other to be the best people we can be.

Prayer

Dear Lord, help us to be strong when we try to improve our behaviour. Give us the courage we need to stand against those who try to tempt us back into our old ways. Help us to see ourselves as friends to those who need our help. Help us to be good, strong friends. Amen.

You could use the Lord's Prayer also.

Thought for the day

Let us remember that we are all members of one community. We need to stand firm and help one another to be our best selves.

Bible verses

Luke 17, v1–14   James 5, v19–20   Galatians 5, v13–15

The truly messy one with the pancakes

Golden Rule

We look after property – We don't waste or damage things.

Preparation

This is a good assembly for Shrove Tuesday, obviously, but it's OK for any time of the year. You just have to be in the mood for a wild and wacky assembly! And it is another one that requires preparation. But this assembly is a winner. I am indebted to Linda Anderson for it. My four children still remember it six years after seeing it. My husband did it again last week and it brought the house down, as always. The important thing is that the message gets remembered.

You will need two tables facing the audience.

Table 1:

- 200 ml milk mixed with 100 ml water
- 100 g plain flour
- pinch of salt
- large egg
- 2 tbs melted butter
- a little butter for frying

In addition you need:

- a camping stove,
- 2 frying pans,
- 2 bowls,

Table 2:

- a box of eggs
- a pot of salt
- a bottle of milk
- a packet of butter

- 2 whisks,
- 2 spoons,
- 1 printed recipe for pancakes,
- 2 volunteer members of staff,
- fire blanket,
- fire extinguisher.

(We never said Linda's assemblies were easy, we said they were good!)

The assembly

You need to start by explaining to the children that lots of people would like to do whatever they wanted, in any way they choose, whenever they choose. For some people, and certainly lots of children, doing that would seem to be the best and easiest way to live.

Rules can seem boring, being organised can seem boring, having to be terribly careful about things can be boring. 'Do as you like, when you like, slapdash, chuck it around, who cares about the mess' seems so much more fun, but it's not how we should live and it's not much fun in the long run.

Then launch into a demonstration, like this:

Take the case of the two pancake cooks. Let's call them Harry and Sally.

> *You need to have the two cooks working at tables, facing the children, much like television cooks. You are the presenter talking them through and commenting on what is going on.*

On this table we have Harry, who is sieving the flour, adding the eggs carefully, gradually incorporating the flour .... (*etc Explain what he is doing as he does it; give it some pizazz!*)

Whilst on this table we have Sally, who is chucking in exactly how much she likes, in the order she fancies, with no thought to the recipe.

> *Go back and forth between the two tables, commentating on what you see. You might care to put an old newspaper under Sally's table! When the two cooks have finished the mixing, light the camping stove and attempt to cook the pancakes.*

If you are in a school hall with kitchen attached, you could cook the pancakes in the kitchen, provided you leave the hatch open and continue commenting as the cooking takes place. You don't want to spoil the pace or the dramatic tension.

When you have cooked some of each cook's mixture, put them on plates and show the children the results.

Now ask for two volunteer children. Get two reasonably quiet, fastidious children. You don't want the joker who is going to say the yucky mess is lovely and eat it with gusto!

Ask them which they would like to eat, attempting to persuade them into eating the yucky one – stop short of force feeding, of course.

Send them back to their places. When the laughter has died down a little, explain the point of the assembly.

It might have seemed a good idea to take the easy way out and be careless, but that cook has failed in two ways:

- First, they have wasted the ingredients and the money they cost.
- Secondly, they have failed to feed anyone with the food, which isn't being very kind.

So we do need rules. They can help make the world a tastier place!

Prayer

Dear Lord, please give us the strength and diligence we need to understand and follow the rules we know we should keep. We do not always manage alone as well as we think we do. Let us not be proud, always trying to do things our way. Instead, help us to listen to you and to know how you would like us to behave. Let us never forget that you love us. Amen.

Thought for the day

Let us remember that we are not always right. Let us remember that rules are usually there for a purpose. Let us also remember that sometimes we should take advice and not be too proud to do as others advise. Let us not think that if we do as we like heedless of others we can still expect things to turn out well for us. Above all, let us remember always to follow the Golden Rules.

Bible verses

Romans 13, v9–10; 12, v16   Proverbs 15, v32
Deuteronomy 8, v6   Leviticus 25, v18–19

We have standards

Golden Rule

This assembly is about how all the rules add up to a good lifestyle.

Preparation

You will need:

- 6 volunteers carrying 6 large pennant-shaped pieces of paper.

I suggest you cut each pennant out of a piece of A3 – coloured sugar paper would be ideal. Each pennant is to have a Golden Rule written on it in big, bold marker pen.

You also need:

- a flag.

You may know a helpful Brownie or Guide leader or the local British Legion may lend you a flag. As an alternative, you could draw a flag on a piece of paper or bring in a book with a big picture of a flag in it. Better still, you could always draw a cross of St George in red marker pen on an old white pillowcase or bit of old sheet, then staple it to a broom handle. (The caretaker will love that!)

The assembly

Show the children the flag or the flag substitute.

If you have a real flag, someone could carry it into the assembly, down the middle of the hall.

Explain why we have flags. Explain that they are called 'standards'.

Knights and kings had standards carried before them so people would know them when they were fighting in a battle. The flag said: 'This is me – I am not ashamed to be here. I am not ashamed to be me.'

We say the same today. We say, for example, 'I have my standards. I do not steal. That is one of my standards. I am not ashamed to say that.'

Just as in the days of knights, we can still know people by their standards. We say some people have high standards. They fly the flag of what they stand for so all can see.

They may fly the flag of:

- CARING FOR THINGS
- KINDNESS
- GENTLENESS
- LISTENING TO OTHERS
- TRUTH
- WORKING HARD

As you say each of these 'standards', ask the child with that Golden Rule pennant to stand up and wave it proudly, then sit down again.

These are our standards. These are the beliefs we share and we are not ashamed of them. Sometimes, like the knights and kings of old, we find ourselves in battlefields.

Questions to the school

Q What do you think you should do if the teacher leaves the class and everyone starts shouting and messing about?

A Carry on working.

When the right answer has been provided, continue:

Yes, because one of our standards is **We work hard.** Stand up if you have the 'We work hard.' pennant.

Go on to ask a relevant question for each rule. When all the pennants are displayed, you can say:

These are our standards – the standards by which people may know us.

There is a well-known poem by Indirjit Singh which says:

> *You cannot choose your Battlefields,*
> *The gods do that for you.*
> *But you can fly a Standard*
> *Where a Standard never flew.*

This means that you can't always choose the situations you find yourself in, but you can always behave in the way you know is right.

At the end of the assembly tell the school that you are going to pin the six pennants onto a noticeboard in the hall.

Explain that you want each of the children in the school to cut out several small pennants and put them in a box in their classroom. When anyone makes a big effort to keep a Golden Rule, they will be able to get a small pennant and write on it their name and what they did to earn the pennant (or ask to have that written on the pennant for them). They can then bring this pennant along to the noticeboard in the hall and pin it next to the appropriate Golden Rule pennant.

In three weeks' time you could have an assembly where you look at the pennants and talk about some of them.

'Let us see if we can fly a standard where a standard never flew.'

Prayer

Dear Lord, help us to be strong and able to do what we know is right. Help us to stand and fly your standard of truth and love. Amen.

Thought for the day

It is not always easy to remember how we should behave. Let us try to remember the Golden Rules at all times and let them guide us.

Bible verses

Ephesians 6, v10–18

Help!
I need rescuing!

Golden Rule

This assembly is about how we get ourselves rescued when we have broken either the Golden Rule 'We are kind and helpful' or 'We are gentle'.

Preparation

All you need is a blank OHP sheet or a clean sheet on a flip chart.

This is definitely a Key Stage 2 assembly. The point is to explain to the children that you can't do things that hurt others and then just put it right with a quick 'Oh, sorry!' The problem of children thinking they either have no way out of a hole, or can get out of it with a quick apology, is a real one and it needs addressing.

I suggest you might do this as a Year 5/6 assembly, or a Year 7 in a middle school.

You might wish to photocopy the RE words, points 1–6, separately and keep the photocopy handy by the OHP.

The assembly

First of all, ask the children if they have ever seen one of those 999 emergency programmes. These programmes always show a major calamity, then someone phones the police or fire brigade and help rushes on its way. They usually end with everyone rejoicing over a wonderful rescue.

Then, tell the school the following:

Well, sometimes we have calamities at school or at home and although we might not be in danger of losing our lives, we are not always sure if we can be rescued.

For example:

- We might have a big problem with our behaviour. We might be in frequent trouble and keep getting told off. We might wish we could be well behaved and everybody's favourite person, but it seems impossible. Perhaps we feel that everyone is convinced we are awful and that nothing will change their minds.
- Or maybe we have fallen out with our friends and we think they will never make up with us. Perhaps a great many bad things have been said and we now feel it would be completely impossible to ever get back to being friends again.
- Maybe we have been very difficult at home and our parents are really cross with us. We would like everyone to be happy again but are worried that this is not going to be possible.

Ask the school for other examples of things that they might need rescuing from. You may know of a situation that is current in school, a spate of bullying or theft or whatever.

Well, we can get rescued but it may take a little while.

Let's think about a real-life sea rescue. *(You can read the following out.)*

Let us imagine we are out sailing, off the coast of Devon, on a warm summer afternoon.

Suddenly we realise our boat has developed a small hole and we know we can't mend it. Calamity!

Quickly we get on the radio and call up the coastguard. They answer and say they are on their way.

Hooray!

But just because they are on the way, that doesn't mean we are rescued yet.

The men have to assemble, the boats must be made ready, maps consulted, boats or helicopters dispatched. Eventually they get to you and then they have to carry out the rescue.

It's a long way from the first phone call to being on dry ground with a mug of sweet tea.

That is a bit like it often is for us. Sometimes, when things have gone wrong and we are in trouble, we want to put things right. But just saying sorry isn't enough. If we just say 'Sorry' and expect everything to be perfect straight away, it's a bit like phoning the emergency services and expecting to be magically out of the boat and onto the land in the time it takes to sweeten the tea.

It's a bit more complicated than that!

So what do we have to do to put things right?

Well, try this …

> *Explain everything we have to do starts with 're-'.*
>
> *Put a big RE as a title on the flip chart or the OHP.*
>
> *Write down the RE words as you come to them. You can cover points 1–3 fairly quickly. Points 4–6 will take some explaining. They are the meat of the assembly.*
>
> *You could get a couple of children to write the following as you come to each point.*

RE words

1. Well, first we have to really wish we hadn't behaved in a certain way. We have to **REGRET** it.
2. Then we have to feel sorry and say sorry that this bad thing has happened. That's **REMORSE**.
3. Then we must decide to put things right. That's **RESOLVE**.
4. Then we have to listen, attentively and respectfully, whilst the people we have upset tell us what they see as having happened and how we have made them feel. After that we have to explain back to them our understanding of what they are telling us. (This is difficult and we must be calm and willing to listen.) When we do this, we **REPHRASE** the content of what they are saying to us and **REFLECT** their feelings back to them. Then they know we understand how they feel. This may take a little time, but this bit is important.
5. Now if we put our side of the story, we will be listened to. We will be **RECEIVED**. (Maybe they will also rephrase and reflect for us.)
6. Now we can make a peace plan together with them, constructing a **REPAIR** kit (or plan) that will suit both sides. We and they can be reconciled gradually and the matter will be put right.

Hooray! We are **RESCUED**! It took a while but, with luck, we are now back on dry land with the cup of sweet tea.

It was a bit of a palaver, wasn't it? Maybe next time we will think more carefully before we speak or act. Let's engage brain before operating mouth!

Prayer

Dear Lord, thank you that you will always forgive us for the bad things that we do. Help us to think about our behaviour towards others, to know when we are behaving badly and to be willing to work hard to put things right. Amen.

or

Dear Lord, the biggest peace plan ever made was by you on Good Friday, when you died so that we might all be rescued. Help us remember that all you really asked in return was that we love you and each other. Amen.

Thought for the day

Help us to remember to try to understand how other people feel before we explain how we feel. Let making a peace plan always be our main intention.

Bible verses

Matthew 18, v19–35
Psalm 107

Chopsticks

Golden Rule

We are kind and helpful – We don't hurt anybody's feelings.

Preparation

You will need:

- 4 lengths of dowelling. Each must be 1 metre long and 1 cm thick (the thickness can vary but the length is crucial – they can be longer than 1 metre, but not shorter).

You also need:

- a plate of chocolate broken into pieces,
- 3 volunteers who are pre-briefed as to the nature of the story. One is a resident in hell and two are residents in heaven. Read through this whole assembly with them before embarking on it. That way they will know what they are supposed to do and whether they are supposed to be cheerful or miserable! Ask them not to spoil the story for the others by talking about it before the assembly.

The assembly

You may know this story. It is fairly well known and makes a good visual assembly.

This assembly is about the Golden Rule 'We are kind and helpful'. To start with I'm going to need a volunteer who likes chocolate. *(Call out the child who is to be the resident in hell.)*

(To the volunteer) It is very simple. You can eat as much of this chocolate as you like, provided ... (you knew there would be a catch, didn't you!) provided you use these long chopsticks to eat it. You can't move the plate off the table and you can't get anyone to help you. It's not going to be so easy, is it?

> *While the child is attempting this (hopefully) impossible task, start telling the story.*

This story is about an old man who had believed in God all his life and had lived a good life, an example to all his community. As he neared the end of his life he wondered what heaven would be like.

> *Keep stopping to check that the child who is trying to eat the chocolate hasn't succeeded. Give them a break after a bit and let them sit down.*

One night in a dream an angel appeared to him. The angel said that, because of his righteous life, he could have a sneak preview of heaven and hell and would be able to see where he fitted in.

The angel first took him to a beautiful garden surrounded by clouds, and in the middle was a table groaning under the weight of wonderful, appetising food.

What sort of food do you think was on it?

> *Take some suggestions from staff as well as children.*

You are all right, and of course there was chocolate – just as our table has.

The old man looked on, amazed. 'This must be heaven,' he said. But it was not.

The angel was slowly shaking his head. 'No. This is hell. You see, the people here can only eat if they remove the food from the table by eating with long chopsticks.'

Sure enough, people started to come to the table and tried to lift food into their mouths. If food dropped off the chopsticks, it disappeared. One person tried to grab food with their hands; again the food disappeared. All the people looked miserable. The old man was greatly saddened by what he saw.

The angel then took him to another place. This place looked exactly the same as the first! In the centre was a table groaning with exactly the same kinds of food!

'This,' said the angel, 'is heaven.'

The old man asked, 'Is that because they don't have to use the long chopsticks to eat?'

'No,' said the angel. 'They have to use exactly the same chopsticks.'

The old man was confused. If the rules were the same, how could this place be heaven? Just then a group of people came up to the table. *(Call out your heaven volunteers.)*

They looked happy and calm and very well fed.

'Ah,' said the angel, 'it's time to eat.'

They picked up the long chopsticks and started to pick up some of the luscious food with them. Instead of trying to cram it into their own mouths as the people in hell had done, they offered it to one another. Everyone was able to eat their fill. They departed content and replete.

Think about what I have told you about the old man. Where do you think he would fit in?

Right, he'll be going to heaven. All his life he had been a good man, who had helped everyone in his community. He'll fit in just fine in heaven, helping other people to eat. And, as it's heaven, someone will help him to eat!

If we always remembered to help each other before ourselves we could all live in heaven on Earth.

But we've got to remember and we've got to do it. We really do have to remember to be kind and helpful.

Prayer

Dear Lord, you told us to love one another as we would like to be loved. Keep this at the front of our minds as we go about our school. Help us to see opportunities to help, and give us the strength to go on helping if we are not always helped back. Amen.

Thought for the day

In our school community we need to be kind and helpful to one another. Let us keep this at the front of our minds as we go about the school. Remembering the rule will make our school a much happier and kinder place to be.

Bible verses

John 13, v34
Matthew 7, v12

Evelyn Glennie

Golden Rule

We listen – We don't interrupt.

Preparation

You will need a CD of music played by Evelyn Glennie. Your local library will probably lend CDs to the school for no charge.

The assembly

Play the music as the children come into the assembly. Don't immediately tell the school the name of the musician; you may have a well-informed child who announces that Evelyn Glennie is deaf before you have a chance to get to the point of the assembly!

Who was listening to the music as we came in?

I am pleased so many of you used your listening skills so well.

This music is fun, isn't it? Does anyone think they have heard this music before? It isn't played that often on the radio or television. But it is very special music, played by someone very special.

I want everyone to listen really carefully. Listen for the timpani.

Let them listen for a minute in silence. A minute can feel like an age, but it won't be unforgiving silence – especially if you don't mind the children bouncing along to the beat.

> *After the time of silence, turn the music down, but not off. I suggest from now on you leave the music playing, just turning the volume up and down.*

I am going to ask you a couple of questions, which you will need to think about as you continue to listen.

The first question is, 'What do you think is the Golden Rule we are thinking about today?'

The next question is this. 'The special person playing the timpani in this music only has four of her senses in good working order. Which sense do you think she might be missing?'

Who can remember what the five senses are?

> *You might like to ask a child to write them down on your flip chart or OHP. You could provide a drawn head and hand for the child to annotate. That will give them visual clues to remind them of the five senses. You don't want the children to be too hung up on remembering them.*

So, this list of senses is your clue.

> *Listen to the music again.*

Well? Which is the Golden Rule?

That's right. 'We listen'.

And which sense is the musician missing?

You don't know, do you? Well, the woman playing the timpani on this record is deaf. Isn't that amazing!

It's true, she is deaf. Now you might think that the rule we are thinking about today is 'We are honest'! But it's true, she's deaf!

You might find it surprising that we are using the example of a deaf person to think about the listening rule. You might find it even more strange that someone who is deaf is able to be a top-class professional musician. It is amazing to think that the woman who is playing on this CD can't hear the music that she is playing.

How, despite not being able to hear, can she work together with other musicians to produce such lovely music?

Being able to listen in the way that Evelyn Glennie does is a real talent. She doesn't just listen with her ears. She listens with some of her other senses too. She uses her eyes and her sense of touch to feel the vibrations made by other musicians and she manages really careful, accurate listening.

Maybe you can now see why she is a good example to go with the rule 'We listen'. She listens with all of her senses. Her senses have allowed her to develop her talent for music.

> *Now turn down the music.*

If we use all our senses to listen, we will be really aware of everything around us.

> *Go back to your picture of the head and the hand, if you have used this.*

1. How can we **listen with our eyes**?
   Discuss how we can look to see if people are happy or sad, we can see if they are not telling us everything or are being brave and hiding their real feelings. If you are the out-going sort, you can do a bit of acting now to make it clearer for the children to understand.

Listening in this way can help us see how people are really feeling.

2. How can we **listen with our hands**?
   Discuss how we can touch another person – for example, on their arm, comfortingly – to show them we are truly listening to them. Talk generally about the body language involved in good listening.

3. How can we **listen with our sense of taste**? Well, we can't! But we can use our mouths. We can listen better by making use of the way we talk to the person we are listening to.
   Discuss how we can ask questions to show we are listening, how we can reflect back sensitively to them what others are saying to us. Talk about how we can affirm others as we speak to them.

   At this point, some clown will say, 'What about our sense of smell?' and you can say that sometimes, when someone tells you something, if you listen carefully you can 'smell a rat'!

So, we might not be as brilliant at listening as Evelyn Glennie is, but we can learn to listen better if we remember, as she does, to use all of our senses.

Prayer

Dear Lord, thank you for listening to our prayers. We know how you would like us to listen to each other: with love and understanding. Help us to use all the gifts you have given us so that we may know how to be good listeners. Help us to listen to others as we would have them listen to us and help us respond with our hearts. Amen.

Thought for the day

When we listen let us try to respond to others appropriately. Most of us have the advantage of our ears to help with our listening. Let us all listen with other senses too and be able to respond with our hearts.

Bible verses

Proverbs 2, v1–9; 21 v13; 1, v23; 17, v17

Turn the other cheek

Golden Rule

We are gentle – We don't hurt others.

Preparation

For this assembly you need some hand lotion, lip balm and a pumice stone.

The assembly

Today the assembly is going to be about hand cream. It might seem like an odd theme for an assembly but it will help you to remember one of our Golden Rules.

> *As you say this, tip some cream onto your hands. Rub it in as you speak to the children.*

When would you or your mum or dad or someone else in the family use hand cream?

Right, when your hands are sore, or your skin is irritated or rough. On goes the hand cream and your hands become smoother and more gentle. That's what this stuff is designed to do.

Same with lip balm, isn't it? You use it for sore lips. When the skin gets flaky and rough, you rub in Vaseline or lip balm to make your lips smooth.

Rough edges on your hands or your lips are simple problems, hand cream or lip balm can sort them out. It's simple and easy.

Has anyone thought about the Golden Rule that must be lurking in this assembly somewhere? I have said a word that gives it away a bit.

> *Let the children guess. Remember that if they suggest a different rule you must say that they have made a sensible suggestion, giving a reason why it was a good suggestion, but then say there is another rule that fits this assembly better. Once a child has guessed 'We are gentle', carry on.*

So, I can keep my hands gentle with hand cream and my lips gentle with lip balm. Sometimes I get hard, rough skin on my feet which I have to use this pumice stone on. I have to work a bit harder on that rough skin.

Sometimes I have to work very hard at being gentle to people, particularly if they haven't been very kind or gentle to me. Just fold your arms if you can think of a time when someone wasn't very nice or kind to you. I can see lots of folded arms, it's quite common, this problem, isn't it?

> *You might want to ask if anyone wants to share their story. Be sure to ask what they felt like doing when they were hurt. If no one volunteers you will have to give a story of your own. I talked about my big sister beating me up, which struck a chord with most of the children. The important thing was that I brought out from the children that they wanted to hurt the person back.*

It seems perfectly reasonable, doesn't it? They hurt me, I'll hurt them. Obvious, really. No need to think about it – or is there? If you have been hurt, it must have been by someone who doesn't know or who had momentarily forgotten the Golden Rules. Just because they chose to ignore or forget the Golden Rules, that isn't really a good enough excuse for you to do the same, is it?

> *Genuinely ask the children this question. You will get children saying, 'If he hits me, I'm going to hit back.' Keep coming back to the Golden Rules. Just because someone else does the wrong thing, should you? Stop this discussion after a few contributions.*

In the New Testament there is some very clear advice about what to do if someone hurts you. Does anyone know what this is?

Someone comes up and hits you in the face. What would you do?

You might want to hit them back, or you might want to swear. Would any of you stand there, turn your head and let them hit your other cheek?

No, I didn't think so. But that is the advice that Jesus gives us.

That is a pretty high standard to manage. It is saying that you do not lower your standards when someone behaves badly. You must set your standards so high that you do not even think about doing anything back when someone has hurt you. Their behaviour is not what controls your behaviour. You can be sure that if someone breaks the Golden Rule, 'We are gentle', you can keep it. You can keep it so well that you do not react or even think about reacting badly.

And remember this hand cream. There is an expression which says that someone who calms down trouble 'pours oil on troubled waters'. Well, you can be someone who rubs a little emotional hand cream into rough situations.

So remember, when people get sore with one another, you can stay gentle and be the soothing cream. You don't have to get rough and make a painful situation worse.

You can now stop rubbing in the hand cream!

Prayer

Dear Lord, when people are cross or unkind to us, please give us the strength to remember that a kind word will turn away anger and give us the courage to do what is gentle. Amen.

Thought for the day

When faced with bad behaviour from others, let us remember to be the best person that we can be, so that we are able to keep our standards high, whatever others choose to do. Our example of good behaviour will help the whole community to keep those high standards of behaviour.

Bible verses

Matthew 5, v39
Luke 6, v27–36
Ephesians 4, v17–32
Proverbs 15, v1
I Peter 3, v8–14

Doing the right thing is the right thing to do

Golden Rule

We work hard – We don't waste our own or others' time.

Preparation

Find two telephones, real if at all possible. If not, a couple of toy ones from Reception or the Nursery will do.

You will also need:

- a pre-briefed volunteer (read the assembly through with the child carefully the day before),
- a road map or OS map (of the locality, if possible; if not, any OS map will do, or even the book of maps from your car – in urban areas, an A–Z is fine).

The assembly

Yesterday evening I got lost. I wanted to go to ... *(name somewhere twenty miles or so away)*. But I couldn't find my map and I made all the wrong choices at the junctions. Each time I got to a roundabout I didn't know which exit to take, at T-junctions I didn't know which way to go and at crossroads I was very confused.

So I stopped at a garage and bought this map. I looked at it, saw where I was and where I wanted to be, and worked out a good route.

If you have a local map, you can hold it up and point to a few places the children will know.

At each roundabout or junction I looked at the map and worked out which was the right way to go.

I really needed the map.

Sometimes we need other sorts of maps to help us with other types of choices.

> *Put down the map and pick up the phones. Call out your volunteer. (Let's call him Mitesh.) Give him one phone; you keep the other. Tell the school that Mitesh's mum has just asked him to tidy his room properly, so she can do the hoovering, because his grandma and grandad are coming to stay tomorrow. It will take about an hour and then it will be bedtime. Pretend to make a phone call to Mitesh.*

'Hello Mitesh. *(Use the child's real name.)* It's … *(Use your real name.)* Do you want to come over to my house? I've got a new Playstation game and we can play it for the last hour before bedtime.'

Q What is Mitesh likely to say?
A *(You should get some answers along the following lines.)* 'Oh, please, Mum'; 'I'll do my room later'; 'Pleeeeeease …'
Q What is Mitesh likely to say if his mum says, 'No – you have to tidy your room'?
A 'It's not fair'; 'You are mean'; 'Oh, please' etc.
Q What should Mitesh do?
A Do the job.

> *Continue as follows.*

Yes, it's rotten, and he doesn't want to do the job, but we have Golden Rules and he knows it's right to work hard and to be kind and helpful.

Sometimes you just have to bite on the bullet and do what is right.

> *Turn back to the telephone.*

'Hello, Mitesh, can you come, then?'

> *The volunteer is primed beforehand to say: 'No, thank you. I'd love to but I have to tidy my room. Perhaps next week after my grandma and grandad have gone home.'*

'OK then, I'll ask William. Bye.'

How does Mitesh feel?

You should get the following answers:
- *Terrible – someone else is going!*
- *Cross with his mum.*
- *Wishes his grandparents weren't coming.*

Would it have been right for his mum to say, 'OK, you go. I'll do your work for you'?

Why not?

We have to learn that sometimes we have to do the right thing – not the easy thing or the pleasant thing, but the right thing. Because doing the right thing is the right thing to do.

But how do we know what is the right thing to do?

We need something to guide our behaviour just as we needed something to guide us to the right place – a sort of map of how to behave.

We have the Golden Rules. If we need to decide which way to go, we only need to consult the map that we have in our hearts and heads at all times.

So when Mitesh's mum asked him to tidy his room and he wanted to go to his friend's, he had to think: 'What shall I do?'

The answer is in the Golden Rules:
- We are kind and helpful.
- We work hard.

Mitesh did the right thing.

Use this to discuss, if you wish, any dilemmas that children face – e.g. playing outside or playing computer games or doing homework.

To make it easier for us we have the Golden Rules posted up all round the school. That means we won't forget them and we can consult them whenever we need to. The map is always to hand!

Prayers

This prayer was written almost 500 years ago. Listen carefully and think what the words mean for us today.

Teach us, good Lord,
To serve you as you deserve,

To give and not to count the cost,
To fight and not to heed the wounds,
To work and not to ask for payment
except the reward of knowing we are doing your work.

Ignatius Loyola, 1548

Dear Lord, you have given us a map of how to behave at all times. Help us to keep this safe in our heads and our hearts. Remind us of this map, Lord, when sometimes we lose our way. Amen.

Thought for the day

Let us remember the Golden Rules at all times. Let us not lose our temper when we are asked to do something we don't want to do. Let us guard against feeling that wc should always be able to do whatever we want to do.

Bible verses

1 John 5, v14
Proverbs 12, v15; 3, v6
Psalms 119, v98; 25, v4

You are unique

Golden Rule

All rules. (Although we live by the same rules, we are all unique.)

Preparation

This does not need much preparation.

You must have something unique. It is easy to pick up a cheap tie-dye scarf. I used a painted silk scarf; a friend used a special tie painted for him by his children. I also used a set of large letters on cards, making up the word UNIQUE, prepared by using some interesting fonts. The Q in the form of a snake went down very well.

You will also need half a dozen different candles – that is, different from one another. See if you can get one of those candles that looks tie dyed, so that you can say this is a totally different, indeed unique candle.

The assembly

When I first came to this school, I wondered how I would ever learn the names of all the children. I can look round now after ... terms/ years and think how many names I know/find I know all of your names. *(How you play this one depends upon how long you have been at the school. You could talk about how many names you have yet to learn, or how many you know. You might say whose name you remembered first.)*

What makes the job easier is a quality that we all have. Can you guess what it is?

Hold the letters out, blank side uppermost, to a child so that they can choose one.

I shouldn't think anyone will guess it from this one letter. How about another couple?

Hold out the letters to the child – or to different children – and get them to choose two more. Let a few children guess if they want to. You never know, they may guess correctly. That will depend upon the letters that are chosen. If the word is not guessed correctly, hand out the rest of the letters and get a child to arrange them into the correct order for UNIQUE.

Does anyone know what the word 'unique' means, now we've discovered it?

Let a few children make guesses. They will probably get to the meaning of the word.

The word can be used in lots of ways. The point is that each one of us is individual and special, bringing our own gifts to this school community.

Let's see; hands up if you are a Manchester United fan. Keep your hand up if you are a Man U fan and like Blue. Keep your hand up if you are a Man U fan who likes Blue and carrots ...

Continue like this until you have one child with their hand up.

We have found a unique set of circumstances that ... *(name of child)* has. But these were on the outside. We are also unique on the inside, in how we feel. The inside feelings are often more difficult to work out than outside ones like 'I support ... *(local)* football team.' It is sometimes hard to say what we are feeling.

All the bits and pieces of feelings, talents, likes, dislikes, ambitions, hopes and disappointments add up to you being unique. There is only one you. No one else feels quite like you, or has exactly your talents. You are one person, unique and different from everyone else.

We all have the potential to do all sorts of things and be all sorts of things.

In this school we expect the best of you, and want all those good bits inside you brought out. That is what we are trying to do. It is easy to see this in the classroom. Teachers ask that you constantly improve your skills and practise them.

Seeing the best of you outside the classroom can be more difficult.

Fortunately, we have the Golden Rules in this school to help you with being the best person that you can be.

Look at all these candles. *(Ask a child to light them or light them yourself.)* All these candles are different. This one was hand made; there isn't another one like it. All these candles have at least one thing in common. The flame.

All of us here live by the same bright flame, the Golden Rules. They light our way to being the best and brightest person we can be. The rules are the same, but they help us to shine out as our best, unique self.

Prayer

Dear Lord, thank you for creating us to be like no one else. Help us to be all that you intend us to be, and let your light shine within us. Amen.

Thought for the day

There are so many different people in this world, making it a fascinating and interesting place to be. All their talents and skills give everyone a chance to make a unique contribution to the world we live in. We must take the chance to be the best that we can be and make our unique and positive contribution.

Bible verses

Colossians 3, v23
Philippians 1, v6; 2, v13
Proverbs 22, v29

The wisdom of Solomon

Golden Rule

We are honest – We don't cover up the truth.

Preparation

This is the only assembly in this book that is explicitly based on a Bible story (1 Kings 3, v16–28).

There is a choice in how you present this. If you have time, it would be effective to rehearse a few children to act out the roles. If there isn't time, use index cards with the lines written on them. You can help the children with the reading, or even tell them their lines.

You will need four volunteers, two girls and two boys. Alternatively, you could have a group of five (at least two of them girls).

You will also need some simple props.

- For the first part of the assembly you need 2 dolls (they need to be the kind that look like realistic babies) and an article of baby clothing. Use something that looks as if it could have sentimental value (not an old nappy). In the story below, the article is a dress.
- For the second part you need 1 of the baby dolls, a crown (use gold paper or card), a cloak and a sword.

The assembly

At the end of this assembly I am going to ask you which Golden Rule the story is about. I think it will be obvious.

Now, depending on time, you can either tell the first story or narrate it with two or three children miming it.

Once upon a time there were two sisters. They both had baby dolls. One doll was called Alice and one was called Bubby. They were very precious to the sisters.

One day, one of the sisters, Amelia, dressed her dolly in one of her old dresses, one that she had worn when she was a baby. The other sister, Mary, wanted the dress for her baby doll. She said it was hers, even though she knew it wasn't really. They argued and argued. Eventually Mum came in. She was very cross. She asked whose baby dress it was. They both said 'Mine'.
'OK,' said Mum. 'You'd better have half each.' And she picked it up, ready to rip it in two.

'No,' screamed Amelia. 'Don't rip it! Give it to Mary, but don't rip it. It's too precious.'

At this, Mum knew whom the dress really belonged to. She gave it back to Amelia. Only the real owner of the dress would be so concerned about it.

Mum knew whom was telling the truth and who was telling a lie. It was a clever idea of Mum's to prepare to rip the dress to find out the truth. She got the idea from a famous person in history, King Solomon. The problem he had was not with a baby's dress but with a BABY!

At this point you need to ask for volunteers, or the group that you have rehearsed: two mothers, King Solomon and a non-speaking guard.

Either take the part of narrator yourself, or (if you have five volunteers) a child can read it.

Narrator: Our story is set thousands of years ago, in a hot country called Israel. The story took place so long ago that they didn't have lots of things that we take for granted. They didn't have television or computers or McDonalds or lots of our modern medicines. These two women both had a baby boy. Sadly, one of the boys died. The mother could not accept that this had happened. She crept to the house next door in the night and secretly swapped the two babies. She changed the baby who had died for the baby who was still alive. Then she crept home with the live baby boy.

While this is being read, the mothers should lie down, each with a doll. One mother mimes sleep. The other cries and then creeps across the floor to the other mother, with her doll. She swaps it with the other doll.

Narrator: When the poor lady next door woke up and found her baby dead, at first she was too grief stricken to do anything but cry. Then she looked again at the child and realised it was not hers. She went outside and saw her neighbour playing with the child that she knew was her own baby. What would you do? Hard to imagine, isn't it?

Some children may guess.

Narrator: There was a terrible fuss. One woman was accusing the other of stealing the baby and no one else knew the children well enough to tell them apart. Fortunately at that time the country was ruled by a very wise king. This king was called Solomon. The case was taken to King Solomon. Both women went before him to plead to be allowed to keep the child.

How dramatic this scene is depends upon the acting ability of the children and the time available. Write their lines on cards if there is no rehearsal time. Make the words as simple or complicated as you like. Once the girls have done their pleading, take up the tale again.

Narrator: The baby was given to the king. He was asked to decide which woman should keep the child. King Solomon listened carefully to what the women said. He thought for a while, then turned to the guard standing behind.

King Solomon: Give me your sword.

The guard hands it over.

King Solomon: There is no way of finding out from anyone else who this baby belongs to. One of these women is not telling the truth. I have no way of knowing who is being truthful, so I have decided that the child will be cut in half and each woman can have one half.

Narrator: A gasp ran round the court. The king must have gone mad. He wasn't as wise as they had thought.

False mother: All right then, if that's what you want to do, do it. Then no one shall have the baby.

Real mother (impassioned): No! Don't kill my child! I'll give up my claim. Let the woman have him to bring up, just don't hurt him.

King Solomon: It is clear to me now who is the real mother of the child. You would have given him up to keep him alive. You were more concerned about the child.

The king hands the baby over to the real mother.

That is the end of the story. Thank you to everyone who helped.

So, which Golden Rule was this assembly about?

Yes, 'We are honest – We don't cover up the truth'.

If children suggest other rules, use their answers constructively.

This case really did seem to be a matter of life and death. Although our lies are usually less dangerous than that woman's lie, they nearly always cause pain and heartache. And one lie often leads to another.

Lying is wrong. It will set us off down a dark, dangerous path. And not everyone we meet will have the wisdom of Solomon and be able to bring the truth into the light.

Prayer

Dear Lord, you know the truth and you let us know when we are lying. Help us to listen to you in our hearts and always say whatever is true. Amen.

Thought for the day

Let us guard our tongues and never think that it is acceptable to say things that are not true. Let us remember that lies destroy other people's confidence in us. Let us remember that we do not know where our little lie may lead.

Bible verses

Psalm 24, v3–5
Matthew 12, v33
I Timothy 1, v19
Proverbs 11, v3
Deuteronomy 5, v20

Fruits of the spirit

Golden Rule

We are gentle – We don't hurt others.

Preparation

You will need two or three pieces of fruit. The important thing is that the fruit have seeds, pips or stones. Any of the following fruit will do:

- apples,
- pears,
- peaches,
- grapes (not seedless),
- tomatoes,
- plums,
- apricots (whole and fresh),
- damsons.

You have to be able to produce six to ten seeds or pips.
  You will also need:

- a green pepper full of seeds (a packet of seeds if a pepper is not available),
- some potting compost in a large pot or several pots (enough to plant the seeds; 2 or 3 to a pot is enough).

The assembly

Bring in the basket of fruit. You should have the pot(s) of compost ready for use. Talk about the fruit and how they grow. Cut open a fruit and show the seeds. Talk about the seeds, explaining that although seeds are small and hidden inside the fruit, they will produce their own fruit eventually. Tell them seeds can only produce their own fruit. Apple pips will make apples, pepper seeds will produce peppers. Show them as you cut – grape seeds, apple seeds (halve the apples), pear seeds, peach stones, avocado stones, whichever you have.

We are a bit like these fruits. We have some good seeds and some bad seeds inside us. What is inside us will eventually grow and show itself.

If we are full of angry thoughts and feelings against others, will we turn out to be a kind friend?

If we think about getting back at people and hitting the ones we don't like, will that grow into gentle actions? No, it won't.

Q If you feel really angry with someone deep inside, what will eventually show? What will you do eventually?

A *Take two or three answers: hit them, be horrible to them etc.*

Yes, angry seeds, even when out of your sight, will eventually produce angry fruit.

We have to have the right seeds to produce the right fruit. We must have the right thoughts and the right words deep inside us.

Look at the fruit again. Cut the pepper and scrape the seeds out (if you are using one). Ask five children to come out and help you to plant the seeds.

If we want to produce a good person, we must plant good thoughts and words.

If we want to have the good fruit showing, we must have the right seeds inside.

For example, if we want to grow into someone who is kind and helpful we should:
- care for our friends *(one child plants a seed)*,
- think about them *(child plants a seed)*,

- notice if they are sad *(child plants a seed)*.

What else? *(Take a couple more suggestions from the floor and ask the remaining two children to plant seeds.)*

If we do these things, we will grow into a kind person.

Today we want to think about being a gentle person.

What should we do? What seeds do we need to have deep inside us to produce a gentle person?

> *Get them started with the following prompts:*
- How about thinking sometimes we might be wrong *(child plants a seed)*?
- Don't think unkind thoughts about others, think kind ones instead *(child plants a seed)*.
- Make friends with our family before we go to sleep *(child plants a seed)*.
- Don't join in gossip *(child plants a seed)*.
- Be prepared to say sorry if we think we may be wrong *(child plants a seed)*.
- Don't say anything if we think it may start trouble later *(child plants a seed)*.
- Notice people when they do kind things and say thank you *(child plants a seed)*.

Seeds, once planted, need:
- warmth,
- water,
- light.

The seeds inside us will grow with:
- affection,
- thanks,
- praise,
- love.

We can give these to each other. Then seeds will grow and the fruit they produce will be a gentle person.

Let us try to think in this week's Circle Times about ways we can behave that will lead us to grow into gentle people.

Now we are going to water these seeds and put them where they will grow.

Prayer

Dear God, plant your spirit in us so we may have love, joy, peace, patience, kindness, goodness, faithfulness, gentleness and self-control. Help these qualities to grow in each of us so we may think and behave in ways that will help each other to grow to be gentle people. Amen.

Thought for the day

Let us all think about ways in which we could become more gentle people. Let us also notice the gentleness in others and help it grow. There is no limit in the world to kindness and gentleness, so let us grow it in abundance.

Bible verses

Galatians 5, v22–6; 6, v7
Proverbs 16, v32
Psalms 141, v3–4
1 Corinthians 13, v4–5
Philippians 4, v8

Who wants to be a millionaire?

Golden Rules

We work hard often needs We are kind and helpful in order to work, and gets even better when you add in We listen.

Preparation

This one needs four bed sheets (single or double, although it's a lot more fun with doubles and it's hysterical with king sized). You can use sheets from home as you are not going to chop them up or slosh paint on them. (But you might want to give them a bit of a wash afterwards!)

You will also need:

- 2 pairs of trainers,
- 4 pre-briefed volunteers.

The assembly

Have your four volunteers up at the front in a line. As you start to speak they can begin smiling and waving like games show competitors.

Good evening, ladies and gentlemen. It's time for another episode of 'Who wants to give their sheets an air?'

Encourage applause.

Yes, ladies and gentlemen, here we have four lucky contestants who all hope to win the magnificent prize of a packet of Polos! *(More applause.)*

Now, these contestants are in two teams. Each team has two players. Step forward the Blue Team. *(Two children step forward waving, giving victory salutes etc.)*

Step forward the Green Team! *(Same procedure as before. You can call the team anything you please – a pun on their names might be good: Tom's Tornados, or Durham Dudes, Watford Warriors, whatever.)*

Now let's get the two teams working. First of all, you each have one of these large sheets that are in a heap on the floor.

Your task is each to take a sheet and fold it up into a neat square. Prizes will only go to perfectly neatly folded sheets. You have two minutes, starting NOW.

> *Now do a bit of jokey commentating. It's very hard for a child to fold a sheet on their own and, with luck, also quite amusing. When we did it we had one teacher in a team and he was worse than useless, which was hilarious! After a while, continue.*

OK, stop! You are not managing too well here, are you? Would you like to ask the audience for help?

> *The team members have been briefed to say 'Yes'.*

OK, then. Audience, these four need your help. Could we please have some suggestions for how the two teams might manage better?

> *The suggestion 'Help each other' should not take long to emerge.*

Teams, do you want to take that advice? Will you help each other?

> *The teams reply 'Yes'.*

OK, then. Off you go!

> *The Green Team work together, and the Blue Team work together.*

Yes, this is much better. We are going to have a result in no time!

> *When they have finished, do some judging.*

Our next challenge is even more tense. Can we have just one member of each team, please. Now, you are each to wear a pair of trainers. Your task is this. You have to do up the laces with one hand tied behind your back.

Set them off again with lots of showbiz pizzazz. After a few hopeless minutes, stop them.

Right, you are not doing too well here. Would you like some help?

The team members have been briefed to say 'Yes'.

Would you like to call out a friend?

The team members respond as before.

OK, then, you may call out a friend to give you some help.

They each call out a friend from the audience, who comes out and helps them. They can use only one hand each. Together they get the shoes done up. At the completion of the task encourage riotous applause. You can then have a grand prize giving to the winning team or give a prize to everyone, depending on how many packets of Polos you can run to. Then they all go back to sit down.

Now what did we learn from that?

Well, perhaps we learned that no matter how hard you are prepared to work:

- you can do some things better if you work with someone else,
- you can solve problems better if you listen to advice.

Prayer

Lord, teach us humility, so that we know that although we can do some things alone we often manage better when we work together. Help us to listen to each other, and also help us to listen to you so we may be the best people we can be, the people you planned us to be. Amen.

Thought for the day

Let us remember that if we listen patiently to advice and we work harmoniously with others then sometimes 1 plus 1 equals 3 (or even more).

Bible verses

Ecclesiastes 4, v9–10
James 1, v5
1 Peter 4, v10–11

In this school we can make a new start every day

Golden Rule

If you break the Golden Rules, you can always start again.

Preparation

You will need:

- 2 white shirts, 1 of which will get totally wrecked (try Lost Property or a charity shop),
- some black paint or a blackened cork, black enough to mark the shirt clearly,
- if you can, get an x-ray – difficult, I know, but it would be good if you could (don't worry if you can't).

You will also need:

- samples of your ways of noting success.

For example, you may have stickers, ink stamps with 'Well done' etc., stars, smiley faces – whatever you stick onto the children's books or jumpers to indicate success.

The assembly

Start by telling the children that a friend of yours recently broke a leg. You may have a child in school who has recently broken a bone whom you can use as an example instead.

Explain how when you hurt your bones you have an x-ray and it means you can see inside a person. If you have an x-ray print, show it at this point.

Now, what would it be like if you could look into a person and see, not their bones, but if they had been a good person?

Well, let's imagine what it might look like.

Get a volunteer up at the front. Put a large white shirt on the volunteer.

Now, let's imagine how the day might go ...

You could get the volunteer to do a bit of acting from now on, or they can just stand there while you stick things all over them.

You come into school and say a cheerful 'Hello' to all your friends. That's kind. *(Put a smiley face or something similar on the shirt.)*

Then you see someone come into your classroom with a model they have made at home. You say, 'What's that?' in a sneery voice and laugh rather unkindly. Well, you broke a rule there – you were not kind. *(Paint or smear a black mark on the shirt.)*

Continue in this way. Each time add a black mark for a broken Golden Rule, say what happened and which rule was broken. Add a sticker or stamp for each good thing, saying which Golden Rule was kept. Keep going until the shirt is covered and it's home time in your story. Aim to have fifteen to twenty mixed good and bad things as a minimum. The volunteer should look a serious mess at the end.)

When ... *(name of child)* went home that night, nobody had to ask what sort of a day they had had. It was written all over them!

But in this school we don't make you stay in that dirty shirt. *(Take the shirt off the child as you continue.)*

We give everyone a fresh start and a clean shirt every day. *(Once the messy shirt is off, put on a clean one.)*

We keep an account of the good things. *(Point to a tree of achievement or flags of standards, dominoes of success etc.)* What about the bad things? We learn to say 'Sorry' and know how to mean it, then we wash the shirt and start afresh, trying a bit harder each day. Every day it's a fresh start, a clean shirt and a new day.

Prayer

Thank you, Lord, for the fresh start you give us every day. You have told us that if we humbly say sorry for the things we have done you will hear us and forgive us. You let us be new every morning and you are always loving and forgiving. Amen.

Thought for the day

Let us remember that things are rarely so bad that we cannot make a fresh start. Let us never forget how incredibly pleased people are when we try afresh to be our best selves. Let us keep the Golden Rules in front of us. If we forget them, let us remember we can always try harder tomorrow.

Bible verses

Lamentations 3, v23
2 Chronicles 7, v14
Mark 3, v28–9
Romans 4, v7
Isaiah 1, v18

The one with the jam and pilchard sandwich

Or we need more joy and less pain – more jam and less pilchard!

Golden Rule

All rules.

Preparation

You need only to prepare a sandwich for this one, but what a sandwich! It should be a jam and pilchard (or sardine or some other rather smelly fish) sandwich. You need to be able to lift up one corner of the sandwich and see good-quality, thick, fruity jam and then lift the other corner of the same sandwich and see the pilchard. Wrap it in foil. You also need a simple poster-size picture of a sandwich.

The assembly

This works well at the start of a new term.

Welcome to the new term. Who had a good holiday? Fold your arms if you saw any friends over the holidays. Nod your heads if you played with them. Smile if you had a good time!

I saw lots of people smiling. There were lots of good memories in your heads then. That makes you feel good inside. I had a lovely time one day. My best friend came over and we chatted and went out for lunch and saw a film. Just remembering it makes me feel good.

In our assembly today we are going to look at our Golden Rules. We are going to remind ourselves of them, and think about how remembering them can help us have lots of those good smiley feelings. We don't always have good smiley feelings, do we? Sometimes we feel and act rather moodily and miserably. At those times we know we need more joy and less pain.

Now I've bought in my lunchtime sandwiches. *(Slowly unwrap your foil covering.)* Nice-looking sandwiches! Moist, wholemeal bread with the seeds and grains in it that I really like. It looks yummy. What do you think is inside them? *(Take suggestions; maybe throw in some weird ideas yourself.)*

Some people were right when they said jam, because when I lift the bread, what can you see? Jam. Lovely thick strawberry jam with plenty of strawberries. *(Adapt as appropriate.)* That's a lovely sandwich filling. No one would mind finding that inside their sandwiches.

But that isn't all of it. On this side, when I lift the bread ... oh dear. Who will shut their eyes and smell this? (Invite a volunteer out.) OK, what do you make of that? It's rather smelly fish. It's pilchard, and a rather elderly pilchard at that! *(Again adapt as necessary.)* Oh dear, not many people would want this for lunch. What a terrible filling!

Remember what I said at the beginning of the assembly about having good feelings inside? That's a bit like the jam inside this sandwich. If it were just a jam sandwich, it would be great, but it's spoiled with this awful fish.

That's a bit like us, isn't it? We'd like to have a life that was all jam – that was all good feelings.

You know that kind of feeling. It's what you get when remembering a good time you had with your friends, doing a really good piece of work, being proud of the way you have behaved, knowing you have been a good friend, getting on well with your brothers and sisters. Those are great feelings.

Sadly, sometimes we feel a bit like the smelly fish. We know we didn't do some work as well as we could, maybe we were unkind to our friends, perhaps we were moody at home. Any of these makes us feel bad inside.

Quite often we end up with a life a bit like this sandwich, good in parts.

In this school we are very lucky. We have the Golden Rules that will help us to find the way to keep the nice jam taste the whole time.

Keeping the Golden Rules will help us to keep the good, jammy feeling inside. We won't have to worry about the smelly fish feeling. Whatever we do, we can use the rules to check our behaviour. If we keep to the rules, we know that we will feel good inside. So we have more joy and less pain – more jam and less pilchard!

It's a funny thing about keeping the rules so you keep the jammy feeling. Once you know how good it feels to be your best person inside, that helps you keep the rules. It's such a lovely way to be that we don't want the smelly fish feeling. So it becomes easier and easier. Keeping the rules helps you to keep the good feeling inside. Keeping the good feeling inside helps you to keep the rules.

Sometimes we do forget the rules and end up feeling bad inside. That doesn't have to last. Wanting the good feeling back will help us to get back to being our best person with the Golden Rules to help.

All those people who folded their arms at the beginning know what this good, jammy feeling is all about. On this poster *(produce the picture of the jam sandwich)* I want to collect names of people who have that good feeling, and to write down what they did to get it. So this week, if you get that jammy feeling when you have done a good piece of work, or you have been a good friend, or you have been very kind, you can come and write your name up here, and what it was you did. I might come along to your class and ask you what happened to give you that good feeling. If there are one or two of you that aren't sure about this feeling, you can go and check with the children on here to find out what they did to get that jammy feeling.

Keep the poster and revisit it in a subsequent assembly no sooner than a couple of weeks' time.

Prayer

Dear Lord, please be with us at all times and give us your guidance in helping us to be our best selves. You gave us the example of your son Jesus Christ, who always followed the right path, even to his death. Our lot is much easier. Listening to your voice inside us guides us to do the right things. Let us go on, from strength to strength, listening to that voice, being the best that we can be at all times. Amen.

Thought for the day

We all can learn to be our best selves. Let us always remember to think about the Golden Rules and use them to guide our behaviour. Let us follow our conscience, that feeling inside that tells us what we should do and how we should behave. Help us to recognise the right path and give us the courage to choose it always.

Bible verses

Proverbs 12, v15
Psalms 119, v98; 25, v4
Romans 8, v1–9
2 Corinthians 3, v18

Follow-up assembly

You will need a sandwich similar to the one that was used in the earlier assembly. This one should have nearly all jam, and just a touch of fish. Put it in a lunch box with a piece of fruit, a yoghurt and a chocolate bar. The poster with all the things that the children wrote on it should also be used. Take it down a week before this follow-up assembly. Pick out some of the things that the children wrote before the assembly. Ask the children concerned about them. If the children will tell everyone in assembly what they did it would be more powerful, but instead you can ask them for permission to explain the reason they wrote their name on the jam sandwich poster.

Here is the lunch that I packed up for today. I'll show you what I'll be tucking into at lunchtime. First, a healthy apple. Anyone else got an apple today? Next a toffee yoghurt. *(Adapt as appropriate.)* I really like toffee flavour. Touch your elbow if toffee is your favourite flavour. Now, I wonder what is in my sandwiches? Any guesses?

Lots of children will remember the earlier jam/fish sandwich. Let them tell you. Then see if they can remember what it meant. If the children are having trouble, prompt them and bring out the fact that it was about the feelings inside.

Today I have nearly all jam because I have been trying really hard and remembering to live by the Golden Rules. My life, like this sandwich, has been much more pleasant. As I eat this sandwich fewer bits will taste horrid. And it's been the same in my life. Lately there have been fewer bits that have left a bad taste in my mouth. How about all of you?

Let's look at this poster.

Here's the poster that people wrote on after the assembly at the beginning of term *(adapt if necessary)*. Children were asked to write their names on it if they got that jammy feeling inside. Let's see what is here. There are a lot of names, which shows that this school has lots of exceptional people in it.

Start the ball rolling by mentioning a couple of things that are written on the poster. Then ask a couple of pre-briefed children to come up to the front and tell the school why their name is on the poster. You will probably need to help them draw out the reasons why they felt good about their action.

Isn't it wonderful how many really thoughtful people we have in this school who are always trying to be their best person? This poster has been down for a week. If your name could have gone on this poster during the last week, put your hand up. Good, lots of children and adults trying to be their best person. Hands down. Aren't we a lucky school!

Prayer

Dear Lord, please be with us at all times and give us your guidance in helping us to be our best selves. You gave us the example of your son Jesus Christ, who always followed the right path, even to his death. Our lot is much easier. Listening to your voice inside us guide us to do the right things. Let us go on, from strength to strength, listening to that voice, being the best that we can be at all times. Amen.

Thought for the day

We all can learn to be our best selves and many of us have been achieving this. The feeling inside us can tell us what we should do and how we should behave, and many of us have learned to follow our conscience. Let us recognise the right path and have the courage always to choose it.

Bible verses

Proverbs 12, v15
Psalms 119, v98; 25 v4
2 Corinthians 3, v18
Romans 8, v1–9

Like yeast in dough

Golden Rule

We are kind and helpful – We don't hurt anybody's feelings.

Preparation

You will need some matzo (unleavened bread). Most big supermarkets stock it. If you really cannot get it, use a cream cracker or a water biscuit (I wouldn't advise this, but it may be your only choice.)

You will also need a standard uncut loaf. If you want to, you can have some other kinds of bread as well.

A few stems of wheat or barley or oats would be good. Lots of places selling dried flowers have these if you are not able to pick some in your area or it is the wrong season. Or you could buy a bag of popping corn and use this to show the maize that gets ground up. Major supermarkets all sell popping corn.

You will also need:

- a large bag of flour (bread flour if possible),
- some yeast (small sachet of dried, or fresh). Sorry, but this is crucial!

If you have an oven close to the hall, it would be worth baking some of those half-cooked rolls so there is a lovely smell of bread cooking. Mixing some yeast with a little milk makes a good smell, too.

The assembly

You will need to adapt what you say in accordance with the materials you have available.

Everyone take a deep breath in. What is that smell?

Yes, it is the smell of bread cooking. What you can smell is the yeast working, ready to make the bread rise. *(Set up a teacher to answer as the children may not know the yeast smell. You never know, though, you may have a child with a mother who bakes her own.)*

It is amazing how that smell has got everywhere in the hall, isn't it?

Does anyone know what we need to make bread? What is the main ingredient? ... Excellent, flour. *(If no answer is forthcoming, use the bag you have as a prompt.)*

Has anyone seen a field of corn growing? *(Hold up ears of corn. Failing this, say 'Most people round here will have seen a field of corn, won't they?')*

The corn gets ground up, and I can go off to a supermarket and get myself a bag of flour ready to make bread. I can mix it up with some water and bake it, then out of the oven would come a lovely loaf. Yes? No?

No is right. Flour and water don't make bread by themselves. I'm missing something. If I used just flour and water I would end up with something like this. *(Show a matzo.)*

Some children here may know about this special kind of bread. *(If you have any Jewish children, ask them to name it; if not, say the name yourself.)*

Would someone like to try a piece? I'm going to ask you to tell everyone in what way it is different from ordinary bread. *(Get a couple of children to try it, and pull out words like 'dry', 'crisp' and 'thin'.)*

This is more like a biscuit than bread.

Most of us have bread like this, don't we? *(Show the uncut loaf and break it to show the soft bread inside.)*

I really like hot, fresh bread. Fold your arms if you do, too.

This bread has yeast added to the mixture to make it rise and become the kind of light, fluffy bread that we are used to.

This bread *(hold up matzo)* has no yeast – it is special bread for Jewish people. It reminds them of a time when God helped them to escape from slavery. They had to go quickly, so they didn't have time to let the bread rise.

To make a loaf of bread like this *(show the standard, uncut loaf)* you must use yeast. That is what makes it rise. You will also need this bag of flour.

How much yeast do you think I need to make all this flour bubble and rise? *(Take a few answers. Again, you may be surprised by finding someone who knows.)*

You only need a small amount, like this. (*Show the fresh yeast or open the sachet and show the dried yeast. At this point you could mix the dry yeast into the flour or crumble the fresh yeast into warm water.*)

This will make all this flour into light, airy bread. It's remarkable how such a little thing can make such a difference – the difference between this thin, dry bread and this fluffy, moist loaf.

> *If you feel strong enough and able enough and life has been treating you kindly lately and you have enough energy, you could mix the loaf at this stage, continuing to mix as you explain the real message of the assembly. (Remember to rub in a bit of butter or margarine.) If, however, you cannot face that, just use the ingredients as props.*

Many of our assemblies have been about the Golden Rules. There is a rule about kindness. Who can tell me what it is?

> *The answer is 'We are kind and helpful – We don't hurt anybody's feelings'.*

Well done! Lots of children are really good at remembering our Golden Rules. That is wonderful to see.

Yes, we are kind; we don't hurt anybody's feelings.

Kindness is like yeast. A little bit of kindness can go a long way.

It changes people from feeling sad and low and flat to feeling happy, cheerful and light. When I'm feeling a bit miserable, having someone do me a simple kindness, like making me a cup of tea, really cheers me up. If I'm feeling really sad, someone doing me the small kindness of smiling at me makes me feel better. Sometimes just thinking about kind people can cheer me up. I know that those kind people are the ones I can think of as my true and real friends.

Some children in this room probably feel that they don't have many friends. That is sad, but I know it happens. If you are one of those children, now is your chance.

You are going to be the yeast of kindness in this school. You are going to find that gradually you will get many more friends. You are going to be kind to everybody.

And other children, those who feel they have lots of friends, now is your chance to help. You are going to be the yeast of kindness to everyone. You don't have just the easy job of being nice to your friends.

You all need to make sure that the yeast gets everywhere. If it doesn't, the loaf won't rise.

Hands up if you think you can be the yeast of kindness in this school community. Remember the bubbling yeast gets everywhere, touching every particle of flour. You will touch everyone with kindness.

This week we are going to have Circle Times about how we can be kind to each other and how we can make each other happier.

Thank you, I'm looking forward to that. Many people will work positively together to make this the kindest school possible. We can help kindness work its magic in school just as the yeast can work its magic in the loaf.

Prayer

Dear God, you have touched the whole world with your loving kindness, just as the yeast touches the whole loaf. We ask for your love to touch each of our hearts. We know that we can make a difference to others by our kindness. Support us as we work together to be the yeast, lightening our school, our family and our community. Amen.

Thought for the day

Our lives have been affected by kindness from many people. We know that we can make a difference to others by our yeast of kindness. Let us help and support one another to be the yeast that will lighten our school, our family and our community.

Bible verses

Matthew 13, v33; 7, v12; 10, v42
Ruth 2, v10–12
1 Corinthians 13, v4
Luke 6, v35
Titus 3, v4–5

The noisy Kim's game

Golden Rule

We listen – We don't interrupt.

Preparation

You need a tray covered with a teacloth. On it put about fifteen unconnected objects – don't scrabble round for things at school. (If the objects are well known, the children will remember them anyway, so don't end up with a ruler, a rubber, a pencil sharpener and so on. Get some bits and pieces from home.)

Provide pencils and paper to write on.

You also need some school musical instruments (loud ones) and an airflow ball.

You also could have some loud music. If you choose something current that the children will sing along to – so much the better. Have this ready to play on a CD or tape player in the hall.

During the assembly you will need to call on several volunteers; one group of four to play Kim's game and a second group of four the same age, one group of four noisy children to play a ball game and one group of uninhibited children to play the instruments loudly.

The assembly

Today's assembly is about listening and the importance of listening. So guess what? I need a few volunteers.

Pick four children. Explain that they will be looking at the objects on the tray for one minute, and that they will have to write down everything they can remember at the end of the minute. (Do not start just yet.)

Next, pick a group of four noisy children. When they have come forward, position them around the players of Kim's game, so they are in the way.

You are going to see how many times you can throw this ball around the group without dropping it. Don't forget to count. (*Tell them not to start yet.*)

Next pick the group of children to play the instruments. Explain that you want them to play really loudly along with the music that is being played. Play the music and get the children playing and moving along to it.

Start the children playing the ball game. When you have got that going and encouraged as much noise as possible in the hall, start Kim's game. Keep talking to the children who are playing Kim's game. Don't let them touch any of the things and keep everything as noisy as possible. After they have concentrated on the objects on the tray for one minute, stop the ball game and the music. It may take a little time to settle everyone down. Then ask the children whe were playing Kim's game to write down their lists individually. Don't read out the lists. There shouldn't be many objects on them!

I'm not surprised that you couldn't do very well at this game. Can anyone think what would have made it easier for these children to concentrate? (*Let the children make suggestions.*)

There are lots of good suggestions there. This time we'll set it up differently. This time there won't be any music or ball games. No one will talk to the people who are playing. I'll let them pick up and touch the things. Now everyone else has to be very quiet. I'll be looking to see which class can be most quiet.

Now choose four different children of the same age as the first group to play the game. Start it quickly because silence is going to be hard to maintain. At the end of the minute get them to write down their lists.

Who thinks it was easier that time? Yes, lots of people do. I think there were some classes who kept quiet really well. I'm not sure who was best but class ... deserve a mention. (*Or make some other suitable comment.*)

These lists are much longer. Obviously because there was quiet and calm, the children could concentrate better.

We have a Golden Rule that says, 'We listen – We don't interrupt'. I think today we have seen why this is such an important rule. Interruptions destroy our ability to learn. If we want to achieve as much as possible, we need to keep this rule.

Prayer

Dear Lord, help us to remember to be kind and quiet and allow people to think calmly when they need to. Help us put others' needs before those of ourselves. Amen.

Thought for the day

Listening is a skill we have to learn. Being able to be quiet and not to interrupt is another skill we need help to learn.

Bible verses

Matthew 7, v12
1 Corinthians 13, v4
Philippians 2, v4
1 Corinthians 10, v24

The one about the three windscreens

Golden Rule

We work hard – We don't waste our own or others' time.

Preparation

This assembly needs to take place during the winter, after a few days of frozen weather.

You will need:

- 3 children to act out the part of the neighbours,
- a kettle,
- an ice scraper.

The children don't need to say anything. They act out their parts as you speak.

The assembly

Today's assembly is based on the rule 'We work hard', but it is also advice about being able to work smart. Sometimes you don't need to work harder; you just need to work smarter.

I need three volunteers to act out this story as I tell it.

> *Choose the three children and give them their parts: Martin, Nisha (female) and Jo. Tell Martin where he needs to go to pretend to drive round the hall to the garages.*

This is Martin, this is Nisha, and this is Jo. All three of these are neighbours of a friend of mine who lives in a flat.

I was staying there during the holidays and saw this happen. I got there on a really cold, wet, miserable evening. The weather forecast was for an overnight freeze, but you didn't need to be told that. It had been the same all week.

I drank a cup of cocoa to warm myself up. We watched the three neighbours come home from work *(indicate the three characters)*. Now it really was terrible weather. All three have garages, but to get to them they have to drive all round the building, get out of the car, open the garage doors, drive in, close the doors and then trudge back round the building to the door of their flat.

Martin arrived home first. We watched him drive in and pause by the front of the building, close to the door to his hallway. After a moment he drove on, round the building to the garages. *(Martin acts this out as you speak.)*

He got out of the car, opened the door, got back into the car, drove into the garage, came out again and shut the doors (which took some time because of the wind) and then walked all round the building, shoulders up, hunched against the cold and drizzle. Poor man, his front door was one of the furthest from the garages.

Next in came Nisha. *(She drives in and stops by you.)* She parked her car right by the door to her hallway. She clearly wasn't going to be bothered to park in her garage. Out she got, and quickly ran into the building.

Jo came home next. *(She drives in and stops by you.)* She did exactly the same as Nisha.

So far we've got Martin working the hardest, but the other two look smarter. Why bother with their garages, after all? I think that question can be answered by what happened the next morning.

It was one of those cold frosty mornings – you know, the kind when you can hardly bear to get out of bed. Fold your arms if you know that kind of morning. Yes, I thought lots of you would. Well, it was definitely one of those mornings. My feet went to the floor and came straight back up. Oh, it was cold! But I had to be up, we had plans to go shopping/go jogging/visit an art gallery/fly to the moon. *(Choose as appropriate, or make up a suitable situation for yourself.)*

Anyway, there we were eating our breakfast. We saw the real fun. Martin, who had done a bit of extra work the night before, came out of his hallway, briskly walked to the garages *(Martin does this as you tell the story)*, opened the door of his, got the car out, shut the garage doors, got back in his car and drove off – immediately.

Nisha came out and looked at her frosted-up windscreen, got out her scraper *(hand her the scraper)* and started energetically on her windscreen.

Jo then came out, looked at her car and went straight back into her flat. A couple of minutes later she came out with this in her hand. *(Give Jo the kettle.)*

Who can guess what happened? She put very hot water on a very cold window. What happened?

Right, the windscreen cracked and shattered. By this time Nisha had managed to get her windows clear. After sympathising briefly with Jo, she had to set out for work. Poor Jo.

She had to call the car glass people. Her car had an airbag which was connected to her windscreen. It took a couple of hours to replace it. She had to leave her keys with another neighbour who wasn't going out and pay for a taxi to get her into work as well paying a lot of money for the windscreen.

So, at first it looked as if Nisha and Jo had got it right. But by the next morning, which of the three had done best? *(Let the children answer, even though it is obvious.)*

Who worked the hardest?

Who had to put in the least effort?

Martin put in a bit of effort the night before and got his reward the next day. Nisha and Jo hadn't put their cars in the garages. Look what happened. Jo tried to take another short cut in the morning. Look what happened then.

Yes, our Golden Rule says 'We work hard'. As you make that rule work for you, think about making sure that your hard work gives you the best result for your efforts.

Prayer

Dear God, as we go through life help us to use our strengths and talents wisely and well. We need to reflect on our lives to learn to be smart with our effort. Grant us self-control so that we work hard in a sensible way, not going for the easy ways out that later make a harder road for us. Amen.

Thought for the day

We need to think through the tasks of our everyday lives, allowing time to reflect on and be smart in our effort. Let us use our strength wisely for maximum impact.

Bible verses

Matthew 13, v20–1
Proverbs 21, v5; 31, v27; 19, v15

A lie has a short life but truth lives for ever

Golden Rule

We are honest – We don't cover up the truth.

Preparation

Preparation this time is minimal.
You need:

- box of about 10 large toy bricks (use either old-fashioned wooden building blocks or pieces of Duplo stuck together to make big 5–7 cm square lumps),
- a willing pre-briefed volunteer,
- a planted member of staff.

The assembly

If you do not own a dog, say the following.

Good morning, school. I am afraid that I haven't got an assembly for you today. You see, the dog ate my notes.

Planted staff member: You haven't got a dog!

If you do have a dog, say the following.

Good morning, school. I haven't got an assembly today because I accidentally lit the fire with the notes.

Plant: It's July (*or 'You haven't got a fire' or whatever is appropriate as an impossible excuse*).

You are right, I haven't got a dog/fire/it is July *(whatever)* and I have got an assembly – so I told a fib, didn't I? Now, if we tell lies we can get ourselves into a dreadful mess.

Sir Walter Scott wrote in a poem called *Marmion*, 'Oh what a tangled web we weave/When first we practise to deceive.' What did he mean by that?

Let's have a volunteer out here to help. *(Remember, it must be a pre-briefed volunteer.)*

Right, Arjoo here is about to tell a lie that he thinks no one will find out about.

Throughout this story, as he tells each lie he sticks a large brick up his jumper. If the volunteer is a big chap with a big jumper it might be a good idea to give him two bricks at a time to increase the discomfort. He has to try to conceal these lies, but the greater the number of lies, the more difficult it becomes to conceal them. Eventually, of course, it all gets too difficult to conceal and the whole lot fall out. Throughout this little drama it is very important that the child looks very uncomfortable and increasingly unhappy as the situation gets more and more painful.

You: **Where did you get those sweets?**

Arjoo: **I found them.** *(Lie – he stuffs a brick up his jumper.)*

You: **Where?**

Arjoo: **Um, in my coat pocket.** *(Lie – another brick up the jumper.)*

You: **I thought you had spent all your pocket money?**

Arjoo: **No, there was some left.** *(Lie – another brick.)*

You: **Well, why did you ask me for 20 pence yesterday?**

Arjoo: **Oh, I didn't remember I had some left.** *(Lie – another brick. It's getting tricky now.)*

You: **Then you should have paid me back when you found it instead of spending it on sweets.**

Arjoo: **Oh, I forgot that you lent me some money.** *(Lie – another brick.)*

You: **Are you telling the truth?**

Arjoo: **Oh yes.** *(Another brick.)*

> *About now he should drop the bricks. If necessary, go on forcing a few more lies. The school needs to see him struggle to conceal the 'lies', and he must be seen to try hard to keep them hidden. It is very important that he drops them out of a genuine inability to go on concealing them. At that point you say the following.*

Now, school, this is what happens when you lie. You tell one lie and think you will get away with it. But one leads to another and another and another until you can't manage – and it all comes out in the end!

Then everybody can see that you have been lying. And you look very silly!

What is more, it is a very uncomfortable business. You know it is wrong and that just makes it more painful and makes you unhappy.

It's always better to be honest. Telling the truth is the right thing to do.

You: **Now, Arjoo, I suggest you make a clean breast of it. Where did you really get the money?**

Arjoo: **I found it on the floor.**

You: **Then you should give it to me, shouldn't you?**

Arjoo: **Yes, I'm sorry. I wish I hadn't started this – things got worse and worse.**

You: **Well, let's get rid of these lies. Then say 'Sorry' and promise never to do such a thing again – it isn't worth it!**

> *Now you must thank your volunteer. Reassure the children that it was only a play and of course your volunteer wouldn't really tell a lie! Then you must give the volunteer a big round of applause.*

So, next time you are tempted to lie about something, remember – it's bound to come out into the open in the end.

And remember that you are going to feel uncomfortable and unhappy until it does. Because lying is wrong.

A famous king called Solomon once said, 'A lie has a short life, but the truth will live for ever.'

It's always best to be honest, because telling the truth is the right thing to do.

Prayer

Dear God, we know that it is wrong to tell lies but sometimes it is hard to be brave enough to tell the truth. Please give us the strength to tell the truth at all times. Amen.

Thought for the day

We know that it is wrong to tell lies, but sometimes it is hard to be brave enough to tell the truth. We need the strength to tell the truth at all times.

Bible verses

Exodus 20, v16
3 John, v3–4.
Psalms 19, v14

You can't get the hair mousse back in the bottle – a bit like the genie and the lamp!

Golden Rule

We are kind and helpful – We don't hurt anybody's feelings.

Preparation

You need only a bottle of hair mousse for this assembly. It must be the kind that is transparent and has clear liquid inside. When you depress the pump this mousse changes from a clear liquid, coming out of the nozzle as foam.

The assembly

How many people have heard of Aladdin? *(Brief discussion about Aladdin. What was the name of the monkey in the film? What was your favourite part?, etc.)*

Who did Aladdin have to help him, apart from the monkey?

That's right, the genie.

Where did the genie live?

Yes, in the magic lamp.

How did Aladdin make the genie appear?

Yes, he rubbed the lamp.

Once he was out, would the genie go back in?

No, you are right. He stayed out.

He was a good genie. But suppose he had been a bad genie, what might have happened? *(Take a few suggestions.)*

Could Aladdin make the genie go back into the bottle if he had wanted to?

No.

If you were Aladdin and you knew there was a genie in a lamp, what would you think about before you rubbed it?

> *Encourage discussion about the need to think imaginatively about the results of our actions. Discuss the importance of using our imaginations to create, and therefore be able to consider, possible consequences of our actions. Very often people do stupid things simply because they lack the imagination to foresee the possible consequences of their thoughts and actions.*

Sometimes we have the same problem. Sometimes we say things that cause harm and unhappiness. Once they are said, they cannot be unsaid.

So we have to be careful that we think before we speak. We have to use our imaginations to think 'If I say this, how might it affect other people?'

Look at this bottle of hair mousse. It looks like water, doesn't it?

You wouldn't believe it could turn into something quite different when it comes out of the bottle. But it can and it does!

When you press the pump it squirts out as foam. *(Demonstrate this.)*

We are not able to turn this back into liquid and get it back into the bottle. Once we have pressed the top and squirted it out, it is foam and that's that!

If we don't want foam all over the place, we must think before we squirt.

It is just the same when we speak. If we don't want to cause trouble, we think before we speak. Because once something is said, it cannot be unsaid.

It is not possible to turn speech back into thought and put it back into your brain, just as it is not possible to turn this foam back into liquid and get it back into this bottle.

> *You can use the bottle of mousse to role play a few undesirable situations. An example follows.*

Imagine that you look at a friend's work and say *(squirt the mousse as you say this)* 'That's not very good, is it?'

How will your friend feel? Pretty miserable?

Yes.

Can you unsay this?

No.

Can you get this mousse back in the bottle?

No!

What would it have been better to have done? To have thought more before you had spoken and then said nothing?

Yes!

Continue to give and take examples from the children of times when speaking without thought hurts others. Each time reinforce the message with the visual image of the hair mousse coming out of the bottle.

So, let us always remember that in order to be kind and helpful and not hurt people's feelings we have to guard our tongues. Let us remember that least said is soonest mended; and also that once the hair mousse is out of the bottle, nothing is going to be able to get it back inside.

Prayer

Dear God, please keep my tongue from saying silly, unkind or thoughtless things. Help me to say things that will bless your name and please you. Please help me use my tongue to make the world a better place. Amen.

Thought for the day

Let us all remember that we must think before we speak – and remember, too, that if we are not sure if something is a good thing to say, it's probably better to stay quiet! Let us check against our Golden Rules, asking 'Is it a kind thing to say?' If it isn't, then let us keep quiet. Remember:

Engage conscience before operating mouth!

Bible verses

Psalms 141, v3; 34, v13

Bibliography

Led to the Lost – the Soul Survivor Songbook (compilers Mike Pilavachi, Matt Redman and Jonathan Stevens), 1999

Touch Points, Tyndale House Publishers, 1996

The Youth Bible, New Century Version, Nelson Word Ltd 1993

Covey, S.R. *The Seven Habits of Highly Effective People*, Simon & Schuster, 1989

De Jonge, J.E. *All Occasion Object Lessons*, Barker Books, 1996

Forster, P. *For Instruction in Righteousness*, Doorposts, 1995

Peterson, E.H. *The Message, the New Testament in Contemporary Language*, 1993

Resources

Training – Jenny Mosley Inset Courses

The following courses are available from a team of highly qualified and experienced consultants who can be contacted through:

Jenny Mosley Consultancies
28a Gloucester Road
Trowbridge
Wiltshire
BA14 0AA
Tel: 01225 767157
Fax: 01225 755631
email: circletime@jennymosley.demon.co.uk
website: www.circle-time.co.uk

Promoting happier lunchtimes
Turn your school round – an introduction
A whole school approach to building self-esteem through Circle Time
Assessing the effectiveness of your self-esteem, anti-bullying and positive behaviour policies
Raising staff morale through team-building
Practical activities to maintain and develop the power of Circle Time

Training support for your workplace

The Jenny Mosley Consultancies' well trained personnel, experienced in all aspects of the Quality Circle Time Model, are available to visit your workplace to give courses and workshops to all your teaching and support staff.

We run both closure and in-school days. In the closure day, all staff, teachers, teaching assistants, lunchtime supervisors and administrative staff are invited to explore how to develop team-building and moral values through Golden Rules, incentives and sanctions, and ideas for happier lunchtimes.

During the in-school day the school does not close and the Quality Circle Time method is demonstrated with whole classes of children, observed by a range of staff. In addition to this, Circle Time meetings are held for lunchtime supervisors and an action plan for the school is considered with key members of staff.

Training the trainer courses

Key people may be trained to go back to their school or their LEA as accredited trainers, responsible for supporting all adults and children in their community through the Jenny Mosley model. For details of on-going courses contact Jenny Mosley Consultancies on 01225 767157.

Quality Circle Time training manuals and resources

Mosley, J. (1998) *More Quality Circle Time*, LDA
Mosley, J. (1998) *Quality Circle Time*, LDA
Mosley, J. (1993) *Turn Your School Round*, LDA
Mosley, J. and Sonnet, H. (2002) *101 Games for Self-Esteem*, LDA
Mosley, J. and Sonnet, H. (2003) *101 Games for Social Skills*, LDA
Mosley, J. and Sonnet, H. (2002) *Making Waves*, LDA
Mosley, J. and Thorp, G. (2002) *All Year Round*, LDA
Mosley, J. and Thorp, G. (2002) *Playground Games*, LDA
Mosley, J. and Thorp, G. (2002) *Playground Notelets*, LDA
Goldthorpe, M. (1998) *Effective IEPs through Circle Time*, LDA
Goldthorpe, M. (1998) *Poems for Circle Time and Literacy Hour*, LDA

Mosley, J. (2000) *Quality Circle Time in Action*, LDA
Mosley, J. (2000) *Quality Circle Time Kit*, LDA
Mosley, J. (1996) *Class Reward Sheets*, LDA
Mosley, J. (1996) *Golden Rules Posters*, LDA
Mosley, J. (1996) *Responsibility Badges*, LDA
Mosley, J. (1996) *Reward Certificates*, LDA
Mosley, J. (1996) *Stickers*, LDA

For information about the full range of Jenny Mosley's books and resources, please ring LDA Customer Services on 0845 120 4776.

The Golden Rules Song